PENNSYLVANIA COLLEGE OF TECHNOLOGY

5 0608 010529

D0074450

EA-HF-2

HELICOPTER MAINTENANCE STUDY GUIDE

By Joseph Schafer

JEPPESEN®
Sanderson Training Products

LIBRARY
Pennsylvania College
of Technology

One College Avenue
Williamsport, PA 17701-5799

© Jeppesen Sanderson, Inc., 1984
All Rights Reserved
ISBN 0-89100-270-7

JS312643B

Chapter I
Helicopters In Use Today

1. The helicopters which are operating in today's fleet represent _____ generations of helicopters.

2. The first helicopter to receive civilian certification is the_____.

3. The Bell 47 helicopter was produced until_____.

4. The various Bell 47 models were equipped with either a _____ or _____ engine.

5. The Bell 47 models have been built in various models with a seating capacity from _____ to_____places.

6. The Bell 47 models have been built for various horsepowers. Of the various models, the model_____has the highest horsepower.

7. The Bell _____ was the first turbine powered Bell helicopter which was built for civilian use.

8. This helicopter was a derivative of the military _____ series of aircraft.

9. The Bell 204 uses either a Lycoming _____ or _____ engine.

10. The Bell 205 series was developed from the_____model.

11. The 205 series has a seating capacity of _____ places.

12. The maximum weight of the 205-A1 was _____ pounds.

13. The Bell 205-A1 uses a Lycoming_____engine.

14. The Bell 206 series of helicopters is best known as the_____.

15. All models of the 206 series use the _____ engine.

16. Depending upon the model, the 206 series has a seating capacity from _____ to

_____ passengers.

17. The Bell 212 was the first _____ turbine helicopter which was produced by Bell.

18. The Bell 212 has a four bladed derivative known as the model _____.

19. The Bell 212 uses a _____ twin pack engine.

20. The Bell 212 has a gross weight of _____ in Catagory "B".

21. The Bell model _____ was built primarily for the corporate helicopter market.

22. The Bell 222 has two _____ Lycoming engines.

23. The Lycoming engine in the 222 is rated at _____ horsepower.

24. The seating capacity of the 222 may be as great as _____ places.

25. The first Hiller helicopter to be certified, was the _____ series.

26. Production of the 12 series Hillers now include both the _____ and the

_____ powered 12E series.

27. The earliest models of the Hiller 12 used a _____ engine.

28. The Hiller _____ has a maximum weight of 3100 pounds.

29. The largest of the Hiller 12s, has a seating capacity of _____ places.

30. The Hiller turbine powered helicopter is the _____.

31. The turbine powered Hiller uses an _____ engine.

32. The FII1100 has a seating capacity of _____ places.

33. The Hughes _____ series of helicopters have been produced in several models.

34. All of the Hughes 269 series of helicopters use a _____ horizontally opposed

engine.

35. The Hughes 269 uses a _____ bladed rotor system.

36. Unlike the Hiller 12 and the Bell 47, the Hughes 269 mounts the engine _____.

37. The Hughes 269 uses an _____ series Lycoming engine.

38. The Hughes 369 models are best known as the _____ series.

39. All Hughes 369 series of helicopters use the _____ series of engines.

40. The Hughes 369 has been manufactured with _____ and _____

bladed main rotors.

41. The Hughes 369D has a maximum speed of _____ knots.

42. One model of the Hughes 369 seats four, while all other models seat _____.

43. The first civilian certified Sikorski helicopter was the _____ model.

44. The first large production of civilian helicopters made by Sikorski was the _____.

45. The S55 helicopter is powered by a _____ engine.

46. The Sikorski S55 had a maximum weight of _____ pounds

47. The S58 helicopter was the civilian counterpart of the _____ _____.

48. The original S58 helicopters were powered by a_____engine.

49. The maximum seating in the S58 is _____ seats

50. Some S58 helicopters were converted to the _____ turbine engine.

51. The S64 was the first helicopter to be built for a _____.

52. The maximum weight of the S64 is_____ pounds.

53. The S76 is built primarily for the _____ helicopter market.

54. The S76 uses two _____ engines.

55. The S76 has a _____ bladed main rotor.

56. The Sikorski S61 is powered by two _____ engines.

57. The S61 R has a maximum weight of _____ pounds.

58. The main rotor of the S61 has _____ blades.

59. The Brantly B2 helicopter is a _____ place helicopter which was first produced in the

late 1950's.

60. The Brantly B2 series use a _____ engine mounted vertically.

3

61. Brantly introduced the model _____ in 1965 which was a five place helicopter.

62. The Enstrom helicopter was first produced in _____.

63. The Enstrom F28 series was produced in _____ different models.

64. The _____ series of Enstroms were derived from the F28 series of helicopters.

65. The Enstrom models all use an _____ series Lycoming engine mounted horizontally.

66. The Vertol 107 helicopter is unique because it utilizes a _____ rotor system.

67. A German import helicopter is the _____.

68. The B0105 uses a _____ rotor system.

69. A French helicopter company which imports helicopters to the U.S., is _____.

70. All of the French imports are _____ powered.

71. The oldest of the French models is the _____.

72. The Alouette is powered by a _____ engine.

73. The Gazelle is a _____ place helicopter aimed primarily for the corporate market.

74. The Gazelle uses one Turbomeca _____ engine.

75. The maximum speed of the Gazelle is _____ knots.

76. The Dauphin is produced in two configurations: one is single engined and the other is _____ engined.

77. The Dauphin is a _____ place helicopter.

78. The largest of the French imports is the _____.

79. The Puma has _____ seats.

80. The "A" Star is the first French helicopter to be powered by a _____ turbine engine.

Chapter II
Principles Of Flight

1. The helicopter is capable of flight in the following maneuvers:

   a. _____

   b. _____

   c. _____

   d. _____

   e. _____

2. Maintenance personnel should have a thorough understanding of flight in order to better perform

   _____practices and also _____.

3. The primary airfoil of the helicopter is the _____.

4. Unlike the fixed wing aircraft, the main rotor produces both _____ and

   _____.

5. The span of the rotor blade is the distance from the _____ to the _____.

6. The chord is an imaginary line from the_____edge to the_____edge.

7. The shape of the airfoil affects its _____.

8. Many helicopters use a _____ airfoil.

9. The_____ airfoil has the same curvature on the top and the bottom of

   the chord line.

10. The_____is the direction of the airflow with respect to the blade.

11. If the blade moves forward horizontally, the relative wind moves _____

    horizontally.

12. The forward moving blade is the_____blade.

13. The rearward moving blade is the _____ blade.

14. The relative wind may be affected by several factors including:

    a. _____

    b. _____

    c. _____

    d. _____

15. The pitch angle is the acute angle between the rotor blade_____ and the

    _____ plane.

16. Movement of the _____ changes the pitch angle.

17. The pitch angle is often confused with the _____.

18. The angle of attack is the acute angle between the _____ of the airfoil

    and the _____.

19. The angle of attack is dependent upon the _____ and the

    _____ angle.

20. Lift is the force produced by the airfoil that is perpendicular to the _____

    and that opposes _____.

21. _____ is the force which tends to resist the airfoil's passage through the air.

22. Drag is the force that tends to slow down the rotor as the _____ is increased.

23. Drag varies as a square of the_____.

24. The_____is an imaginary point where the result of all the aero-

    dynamic forces of the airfoil are considered to be concentrated.

25. Movement of the _____ is common on most airfoils.

26. This movement could cause_____on a helicopter rotor.

27. The symmetrical airfoil has very little movement of the _____.

28. _____is the condition under which the streamline airflow separates from the

    camber of the_____ and _____ occurs.

29. The _____ is increased with the angle of attack until the _____ angle is reached.

30. When the pitch angle is increased, _____ must be added in order to maintain the velocity of the blade.

31. Lift will vary with the _____ of the air.

32. Air density is affected by:

    a. _____

    b. _____

    c. _____

33. A helicopter is often capable of hover at sea level but not at high _____.

34. On a _____ _____ more power is required to maintain lift than on a_____ ___

_____.

35. The heavier the helicopter is, the greater will be the_____angle and

_____ requirement to hover.

36. _____ is the force moving the helicopter in the desired direction.

37. _____ must be greater than _____ in order to move the helicopter.

38. Rotor _____ occurs when the rotor is at rest.

39. _____force is the force which straightens the rotor blades while in motion.

40. The _____ and _____ force cause the rotor to cone when pitch is applied.

41. The _____ angle is affected by the weight of the helicopter.

42. The blade tips will pass through a circular surface formed by the rotor blades. This circular plane is known as the _____ or the tip _____.

43. The rotor system will not only produce lift but also produces_____.

44. _____ is obtained by movement of the tip path plane.

45. The rotor disc is tilted_____in order to obtain forward flight.

46. The movement of the rotor disc is obtained by changing the _____.

47. All rotor heads have provisions for the rotor blades to pivot about the _____

    axis.

48. Pitch change may be accomplished by the movement of the _____ control.

49. This movement changes the pitch of each rotor blade an _____ amount.

50. The movement of each individual blade is accomplished by the _____ control.

51. If the lift is increased at one point and decreased at another point, 180 degrees apart, the rotor disc

    will _____ .

52. The rotor disc has the same properties as any other rotating _____.

53. One of these properties is _____.

54. When a force is applied to the moving rotor, the reaction will occur _____ later

    in the same direction as rotation.

55. Because of gyroscopic precession, the inputs to the cyclic are not located on the _____

    _____ assembly where the action is to occur.

56. Torque is developed by the main rotor which is in concurrance with _____

    law.

57. The reaction to torque is a tendency for the fuselage to pivot in the opposite direction of the_____.

58. Several designs have been tried in order to counteract this tendency. These include:

    a. _____

    b. _____

    c. _____

    d. _____

    e. _____

59. Today, most helicopters make use of a main rotor and a_____ to counteract torque.

60. Directional control of the fuselage is obtained by use of the_____.

61. This directional control is obtained by moving _____ which in turn change the _____ of the tail rotor.

62. One of the disadvantages of the tail rotor is the amount of _____ required from the engine.

63. The purpose of the _____, which is used on may helicopters, is to reduce the power required by the tail rotor in forward flight.

64. The speed at which the rotor moves through the air _____ the same on all parts of the rotor.

65. The fastest portion of the rotor is at the _____ of the rotor blade and the slowest portion is at the _____.

66. _____ is built into the blade in order to improve the lift characteristics of the blade.

67. The slower portion of the blade has a greater _____ built into the blade than the _____ portions.

68. In forward flight, the _____ half of the rotor disc moves faster than the _____ half of the disc.

69. The advancing half of the disc will produce more _____ than the retreating half in forward flight.

70. The difference in lift produced by the rotor disc is referred to as _____ of lift.

71. In order to correct for the difference in lift, the rotor must be provided with a _____ _____ on some rotor systems.

72. Two bladed rotors often use the _____ systems to correct for dissymetry of lift.

73. Either of the above mentioned systems will allow the advancing blade to move _____.

74. Corriolis effect causes the shortest blade to _____ because of the blade flapping action.

9

75. This effect will cause _____ imbalance of the rotor system if not corrected.

76. To correct for the corriolis effect, rotors with flapping hinges must also have _____ _____ hinges.

77. This hinge allows the blade to move about the _____ axis.

78. Because of the hinge, the advancing blade will move_____.

79. This blade movement is caused by the shift in the location of the_____ closer to the hub axis.

80. The retreating blade will move _____ when the advancing blade moves forward.

81. In order for the movement of the lead-lag hinge to be smooth,_____are used.

82. Rotors using the seesaw action do not use the lead-lag hinge because they are _____ _____ which reduces the center of gravity shift.

83. The_____on two bladed rotors are usually quite long and mounted with _____ between the rotor and airframe to absorb any_____ _____ imbalance which may occur.

84. The three types of rotor heads which are used today are:

    a. _____

    b. _____

    c. _____

85. The two most widely used rotors are the_____and the_____ _____.

86. The _____ rotor has a feathering axis only.

87. The production helicopter that uses the rigid rotor depends upon the rotor blade to provide the _____ and _____ action to the rotor.

88. The semi rigid rotor utilizes a _____ axis and the blades _____ _____ as unit.

10

89. Some semi rigid rotors have a correction factor for _____ built into the swashplate.

90. The fully articulated rotor system utilizes a _____ axis, a _____ _____ for each blade and a _____ hinge.

91. Certain advantages and disadvantages are present in both rotor systems. List these below:

SEMI-RIGID ROTOR SYSTEM:

    a. _____

    b. _____

    c. _____

FULLY ARTICULATED SYSTEM:

    a. _____

    b. _____

    c. _____

92. Translating tendency is a tendency for the whole helicopter to drift in the direction of the _____ _____.

93. Translating tendency may be corrected by:

    a. _____

    b. _____

94. Ground effect occurs when the helicopter is within _____ of the rotor diameter from the ground.

95. During ground effect, the air becomes more _____ and forms an _____ under the helicopter.

96. Ground effect will be lost when 3 to 5 mph of _____ is obtained.

97. Translational lift is an _____ lift obtained by forward speed.

98. This lift is obtained by _____ of the rotor system in forward flight.

99. Translational lift is noticeable at around _____ mph of forward speed.

11

100. As speed increases, much of the translational lift is cancelled by the _____.

_____.

101. Transverse flow effect occurs when forward _____ begins.

102. During the transverse flow effect, the air at the rear of the disc has a higher _____

_____ angle than the front portion of the disc.

103. Greater lift is created at the _____ of the disc by transverse flow.

104. On semi rigid rotors, transverse flow causes a _____ and

_____ feedback.

105. Transverse flow occurs when the rotor blades are in a _____ and _____ position.

106. Transverse flow is less noticeable on fully articulated rotors because of the _____

_____.

107. The _____ of the helicopter rotor blade are quite different

from the fixed wing aircraft.

108. An airfoil may stall due to:

a. _____

b. _____

c. _____

109. In forward flight, the advancing blade moves _____ than the

retreating blade.

110. The retreating blade will increase the _____ at the tips in high speed

flight due to the inflow of air to the rotor.

111. Blade stall is more likely to occur under _____ loads than under light loads.

112. Stall may occur at rather low operating speeds when factors such as _____,

_____ and _____ are considered.

113. When stall first occurs, only the first few inches of the tip of the _____

blade are involved.

12

114. The first indication of a stall is a _____ as the blades pass through the stall region.

115. When the stall progresses, the nose of the helicopter will _____ due to gyroscopic precession.

116. When a stall is experienced, one should:

   a. _____

   b. _____

   c. _____

117. Autorotation is the process of producing _____ with the rotor blades as they freely rotate as a result of _____ through the rotor system.

118. During normal operation, the airflow through the rotor is in a _____ direction.

119. During autorotation, the airflow is in an _____ direction.

120. The autorotation region of the rotor disc is an area of _____ of the blade.

121. The _____ region of the rotor tends to slow down the rotor system due to a small _____ .

122. During autorotation, the rotor _____ must be controlled.

123. During autorotaion, the greatest amount of lift may be produced in a _____ with the cyclic moved _____ .

124. The success of an autorotation is dependent on _____ and _____ _____ .

125. At a hover, an altitude of 150 feet would be an _____ altitude for a successful autorotation.

126. Autorotation characteristics are affected by:

   a. _____

   b. _____

127. Ground resonance is a _____ vibration which occurs on the ground.

128. If ground resonance is not corrected, it may _____ the helicopter.

129. Ground resonance is associated with a _____ rotor head.

130. During ground resonance, the rotor blades are in an abnormal position in relation to the _____ _____ axis.

131. This condition moves the _____ from the center of the rotor disc.

132. Ground resonance can be aggrevated by:

    a. _____

    b. _____

    c. _____

133. The corrective action for ground resonance is_____.

134. When something is statically stable, it will return to its original position after being_____ _____.

135. When something is statically unstable, it will continue to_____ of the disturbance.

136. Dynamic stability is a term used to describe the_____ of the object after the disturbance.

137. The helicopter is usually described as statically _____ and dynamically _____.

138. Three basic items contribute to the dynamic instability of the helicopter. These include:

    a. _____

    b. _____

    c. _____
       _____

139. To correct for dynamic instability, Bell helicopters sometimes use a _____ _____.

140. By using the Bell method, the rotor head remains _____ of the mast.

141. The offset hinge is another method used to correct for _____ on fully articulated rotors.

142. The basic controls that are used to control flight are:

    a. _____

    b. _____

    c. _____

143. The purpose of the collective is primarily an _____ control.

144. The collective often has additional linkage attached, to _____ engine power as it is raised.

145. On reciprocating engine aircraft, this additional linkage works in conjunction with a _____ _____ box.

146. Free turbine powered helicopters often use a _____ to maintain the proper relationship of the blade pitch and engine power.

147. The anti-torque pedals change the _____ of the tail rotor.

148. The highest positive pitch is required during _____.

149. Positive pitch is added by depressing _____ pedal on U.S. helicopters.

150. In addition to torque correction, the tail rotor pitch is used for _____ control.

151. Two methods used to unload the tail rotor in flight are:

    a. _____

    b. _____

152. The cyclic control is used to tilt the _____ of each individual rotor blade.

153. The tilt is accomplished by changing the _____ of each individual rotor blade.

154. The pitch change occurs 90 degrees prior to the desired action because of _____ _____.

155. The cyclic linkage is sometimes connected to a _____ as well as the rotor control.

Chapter III
Documentation, Publications, And Historical Records

1. Much of the paperwork which is used for helicopters is the same as that used on _____ _____ aircraft.

2. Helicopters usually have _____ paperwork requirements compared to the fixed wing aircraft.

3. The Federal Air Regulations which pertain to rotary wing aircraft, are FAR _____ and FAR _____.

4. Of these regulations, FAR 29 pertains to _____ category only.

5. Many of the FAR's do not deal specifically with helicopters but contain _____ information pertaining to helicopters.

6. The use of manuals by technicians performing helicopter maintenance is covered in FAR _____ _____.

7. Type cerificate data sheets often carry information concerning the _____ life of various components.

8. Most Data Sheets have a note stating: _____ _____ _____.

9. The airworthiness certificate is valid as long as _____ _____.

10. All aircraft are required to carry a current Weight and Balance List and an _____ _____.

11. The equipment contained on may older helicopters varies because of updating through:

a. _____

b. _____

c. _____

12. All helicopters are required to have a _____ schedule.

13. This schedule is a _____ record of all components which have a finate life.

14. The lives of _____ items may be increased or decreased as information is gathered relating to failures.

15. The responsibility of these records is that of the _____.

16. These records are usually updated by the _____.

17. If retirement schedules are lost or destroyed, the component must be _____.

18. Three basic methods are used to keep retirement schedules. These are:

a. _____

b. _____

c. _____

19. The method of record keeping which is to be used is usually based upon the number of _____ _____ and the number of spare _____ used to support the helicopters.

20. A retirement schedule must contain the following information:

a. _____

b. _____

c. _____

d. _____

e. _____

f. _____

21. Using the card method, one card is required for each _____ that has a finate life.

22. Often the computor system of record keeping includes not only the components with finate lives, but a record of reoccurring _____ notes.

23. In addition to a retirement schedule, a recommended _____ schedule is kept on the various components.

24. Often these two records are kept as _____ record.

25. Information on the life of the components may be found in the manufacturer's _____ _____ manual.

26. Using the schedule below, fine the correct time for replacing the Main Rotor Yoke. It is _____ _____ Aircraft TT.

Bell Helicopter, Model D-1
Serial #476, N2215
Date of Mfg., June 1952

COMPONENT TIMES and OVERHAUL
or RETIREMENT SCHEDULE
DATE 4-12-78   A/C   TT 3828.5 Hrs.

COMPONENT	ACFT TT WHEN NEW	ACFT TT WHEN LAST OVERHAULED	REPLACE OR OVERHAUL ACFT TT	TACH TIME
M/R Hub yoke 47-120-177-1	2731.5	3739.2	6331.5	3343.3
Inspect	NA	NA	4339.2	1351.0
M/R Grip S.N. SR-01017 47-120-135-5	3828.5	NA	6328.5	3354.6
Inspect	NA	NA	4339.2	1351.0
M/R Grip S.N. SR-00953 47-120-135-5	3828.5	NA	6328.5	3354.6
Inspect	NA	NA	4339.2	1351.0
Gimble Ring S.N. RE-1505 47-120-014-023	3828.5	NA	5028.5	2054.6
Inspect	NA	NA	4339.2	1351.0
Mast 47-130-114-7	1967.8	3739.2	Unlimited	
Inspect	NA	NA	4339.2	1351.0
Mast Controls	2903.3	3739.2	Unlimited	
Inspect	NA	NA	4339.2	1351.0
T/R Blade Grip Retaining Bolts 47-641-194-1	3828.5	NA	4428.5	1454.6
Inspect	NA	NA	4339.5	1351.0
T/R Hub yoke S.N. N29-1395 (34 Hr. since new when installed)	3828.5	NA	4194.5	1220.6

T/R Shafting (R) 47-644-187-17 (F) 47-644-180- 9 (M) 47-644-180-11	3739.2	NA	Unlimited	
Inspect	NA	NA	4339.2	1351.0
T/R Gear box 47-640-044-7	2848.5	3739.2	Unlimited	
Inspect	NA	NA	4039.2	1051.0
T/R Blades 47-642-102-49	3739.2	NA	4339.2	1351.0
Inspect	NA	NA	4039.2	1051.0
Engine YO-355-5 S.N. E-590135 (7 Hr. since new when installed)	3828.5	NA	4421.5	1447.6
Fan Belts 47-661-041-3	3828.5	NA	4728.5	1754.6
Inspect (Check tension every 50 hrs.)				
Transmission 47-620-600-5	------	3739.2	4339.2	1351.0
Inspect (Inspect clutch shoes at 300 hr.)				
Engine Mount 47-612-135-1	2988.2	3739.2	5488.2	2500.0
Inspect	NA	NA	4039.2	1051.0

27. Using the same schedule, find the aircraft time when the Main Rotor Grips were installed. It was at

   A/C TT _____ hr.

28. The next major inspection of the main rotor grips is due at A/C TT _____ hrs.

29. Using the same schedule, determine if the T/R Hub Yoke was new when it was installed. It _____

   _____ new.

30. Using the same schedule, what is the life of the tail rotor shafting? _____ _____ .

31. Using the same schedule, what is the finate life of the tail rotor blades? _____ hrs.

32. Using the same schedule, how often must the clutch shoes be inspected? _____ hrs.

33. Records of Service Bulletins and AD Notes may be kept in the logs or may be found on a _____

   _____ as well as the log.

34. Many large operators use logs which have _____ copies that are returned to the

   maintenance headquarters.

35. The purpose of multiple copy logs is: _____

   _____

   _____ .

36. Sometimes additional log pages are sent to the _____ of the aircraft for product support planning.

37. Computorized maintnance is sometimes done by separate _____ specializing in this type or work.

38. Most new helicopters have maintenance publications written which use the _____ standardized format.

39. Older aircraft usually uses a _____ format which is usually derived from the military system.

40. The operator's manual is sometimes referred to as the _____ manual.

41. The first section of the operator's manual contains the helicopter operating _____ _____.

42. The operating r.p.m. would be contained in the _____ section of this manual.

43. The _____ section of the operating manual would contain procedures.

44. The performance charts would be found in the _____ section of the operator's manual.

45. The starting procedures would be found in the _____ section of the operating manual.

46. If helicopter loading instructions were needed, these could be found in the _____ section of the operator's manual.

47. The _____ section of the operator's manual contains information on other than the standard configuration models of the helicopter.

48. The maintenance manuals are written in two basic formats which are:

_____ and the

_____ .

49. Most new helicopters follow the _____ format.

50. Information contained in the maintenance manual varies. The most complete manual would contain field _____ instruction and _____ instructions in the same manual.

51. Some manufacturers have only _____ maintenance contained in the manual.

52. Overhaul instructions are often not contained in the maintenance manual because of the amount of _____ necessary to perform the various overhaul tasks.

53. Some companies have _____ programs for various components rather than field overhauls.

54. The use of _____ for maintenance manuals reduces storage space and aids in the revision of the manual.

55. All manufacturers have a revision service on maintenance manual. This is usually done through a _____ to the revisions.

56. Following the old format, information of a general nature would be found in the _____ _____ section of the manual.

57. Some chapters may contain two of the same sections when more than one type of _____ _____ is used on the helicopter.

58. Each section of the old format is broken down into the following areas:

    a. _____

    b. _____

    c. _____

    d. _____

    e. _____

    f. _____

59. Using the ATA system, each _____ is assigned a number representing a section of the manual.

60. This ATA numbering system remains the same regardless of the _____ or _____ of the helicopter.

61. Any systems not contained on a specific helicopter would result in a deletion of that _____ _____ number in the maintenance manual.

62. In addition to the chapter number of the system, other digits are added to cover the _____ _____ or subsystems of the system.

63. The ATA system uses a digit system to cover each:

    a. _____

    b. _____

    c. _____

64. The illustrated parts breakdown or "I.P.B." may also be found in _____ basic formats.

65. Using the old format, the first section of the I.P.B. contains information on:

    a. _____

    b. _____

    c. _____

    d. _____

66. Warranty information would be contained in the _____ section of the I.P.B.

67. There are always _____ page numbers between illustrations in the I.P.B.

68. At the beginning of each section, the first illustration contains large assemblies. The preceeding illustrations show _____ of the large components.

69. Each text page is marked as to the _____ number that the text is referring to.

70. The specific number of a part needed for assembly would be contained in the _____ column of the text page.

71. If a particualr component was used on more than one model, this information would be contained in the model _____ column of the text page.

72. When only the part number is known, the location of the part may be located by using the _____ _____ in the back of the IPB.

73. The ATA I.P.B. is written on the same format as the _____ manual with a number assigned to each system.

74. Service Bulletins contain additional information regarding the _____

    of the helicopter.

75. Service Bulletins are usually the direct result of _____

    _____ or improvements as required by such problems.

76. Service Bulletins often become _____ if the matter

    is considered serious.

77. Service Bulletins are available by subscription from the _____ .

78. In addition to Service Bulletins, some manufacturers furnish _____ or

    technical bulletins.

79. Service letters contain information that is beneficial to the _____ but does not

    directly affect the airworthiness of the helicopter.

80. Service Instructions are usually associated with _____ of the

    helicopter with kits.

81. Supplemental Type Certificates are issued by the _____ for modifications.

82. An STC may be obtained by the original manufacturer or _____ who modifies

    an aircraft and receives approval.

Chapter IV
Basic Helicopter Maintenance

1. The right and left hand side of the helicopter are determined by viewing the helicopter from the _____ looking forward.

2. The pilot is often located on the _____ hand side of the helicopter.

3. Such items as rotor blades are often _____ coded because of the many rotating components.

4. On semi rigid rotors, the colors _____ and _____ are often used.

5. Many helicopters are equiped with _____ gear rather than wheeled landing gear.

6. Ground handling wheels necessitate several safety precautions:

    a. _____

    b. _____

    c. _____

    d. _____

    e. _____

    f. _____

7. An _____ and _____ pressure is often required when moving a helicopter on ground handling wheels.

8. Some helicopters are landed on a _____ to provide ease in ground handling.

9. Certain precautions must be observed when moving helicopters with a towbar which include:

   a. _____

   b. _____

   c. _____

   d. _____

10. Helicopters should always be parked facing the _____ wind.

11. If the helicopter is equiped with skidgear, it should be parked with the wheels _____

    _____.

12. Many helicopters are equiped with tiedowns on the fuselage which also often serve as the_____

    _____.

13. Anytime the helicopter is parked, the main _____ must be tied down.

14. Blade tiedowns must be tight enough to prevent blade _____.

15. Most turbine powered helicopters have covers for the _____ and

    the _____ of the turbine engine.

16. The _____ is the usual lifting point when the whole helicopter requires lifting.

17. Large components on the helicopter are usually provided with _____

    for the removal of the component.

18. When leveling the helicopter, it is jacked up on special _____ which are

    provided for that purpose.

19. A formula must be used when _____ are used on the torque wrench.

20. Some manufacturers place the torque _____ on the special tool to be used.

21. Bearings are used to carry _____ loads as well as rotational and oscillating

    loads.

22. Fill in the common terminology on the bearing shown below:

a. _____

b. _____

c. _____

d. _____

e. _____

f. _____

g. _____

STRAIGHT ROLLER BEARING

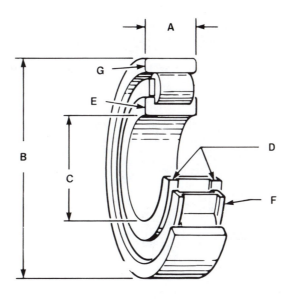

23. The cages used in bearings vary depending upon the application and _____.

24. Bearings carrying an airframe manufacturer's part number _____ be substituted with any other bearing.

25. The most widely used bearings in helicopters is the _____bearing.

26. The roller bearing is normally associated with _____ loads.

27. Some roller bearings are capable of carrying thrust loads of slow rotational speeds that are _____ _____ roller bearings.

28. The needle roller bearing is used to carry _____ radial loads.

29. Spherical bearings are often found in _____ linkage.

30. Spherical bearings may be lubricated by:

    a. _____

    b. _____

31. Spherical bearings used on rod ends often have a _____ portion for rigging adjustment.

32. When replacing rod ends, the actual length of the control rod is sometimes determined by the use of a _____.

33. Rod ends must be properly _____ in order to prevent binding in the control system.

34. Some spherical bearings are held in place by a special process called _____.

35. This process involves the use of a sleeve which is _____ to hold the bearing in place.

36. The _____ of bearings is probably the greatest contributing factor to the life of the bearing.

37. Bearings that are shielded on both sides are lubricated by _____ held in the bearing itself.

38. Greases may be classified as _____ temperature and _____ temperature.

39. The temperature of the grease is dependent upon the _____ temperature of the bearing.

40. Bearings requiring oil lubricant may use _____, _____ or pressure as the source of lubricant.

41. A typical area using a spray system may be the _____ which often includes its own oil system.

42. Areas which hold oil for lubrication often make use of a _____ for visual inspection of the oil lever.

43. Lubrication charts for helicopters denote the type of _____ the _____, and the _____.

44. If bearings are to be removed and reinstalled, it is most important that the area surrounding the bearing be _____ _____ in order to protect the bearing from dirt.

45. The preferred method of removeing bearings is by the use of an _____.

46. The use of hammers directly on the races is considered a poor _____ practice because the races may easily be chipped.

47. When pressing bearings off a shaft, the _____ race should always be supported.

48. Discoloration of the bearing is always an indication of excessive _____. This may be caused by a lack of lubrication.

49. Two bearings specifically made to work in the conjunction with each other are called _____ bearings.

50. The proper installation of these bearings is determined by a _____ inscribed on the outer races.

51. The load on a ball bearing in regards to thrust is sometimes indicated by _____ inscribed on the outer race.

52. Bearings used on conjunction with each other may be stacked in _____, _____ or _____.

29

53. Label the bearing in the figure as to the correct stack up:

a. _____

b. _____

c. _____

54. The _____ stack can carry thrust loads in one direction only.

55. The _____ or _____ method

can carry thrust loads in both directions.

56. The _____ method would be used if the outer racewere to be

held stationary.

57. In some special installations, bearings are heated in an _____ for easier installation.

58. When the outer race is not to turn often an _____ or

_____ fit is required.

59. In the figure below, how much shim will be required to obtain a .004 pinch?

_____ .

SHIM PEALED TO THICKNESS DESIRED

BEARING CAP
HELD DOWN
FIRMLY

FEELER
GAUGE
USED TO
DETERMINE
SHIM THICKNESS

OUTER
RACE

BALL BEARING   HOUSING →

EXAMPLE: FEELER THICKNESS   .030
             PINCHED DESIRED   .004
                                   ————
             SHIM THICKNESS

60. One of the latest types of bearings to be used in the helicopter is the _____

bearing.

61. This type of bearing cannot carry _____ loads but can carry oscillating

loads.

62. These bearings are in wide usage on the _____ of the newer helicopters.

30

63. The rubber in the bearing acts as the _____ eliminating the need for oil or grease.

64. With the use of _____ rubber, the characteristics may be altered to meet different demands.

65. The basic construction of these bearings consists of layers of _____ and _____.

66. These laminates may be used to form various bearings to include:

    a. _____

    b. _____

    c. _____

    d. _____

    e. _____

67. Some of the advantages of this type of bearing are:

    a. _____

    b. _____

    c. _____

    d. _____

    e. _____

    f. _____

    g. _____

    h. _____

68. The disadvantages of this type of bearing are _____ and _____.

69. These bearings may be used to provide blade _____, restrain, and pitch _____ on semi-_____ rotor systems.

70. Gears are used to:

    a. _____

    b. _____

    c. _____

71. Gears are often classified by the type of teeth used. The most common types would be:

   a. _____

   b. _____

   c. _____

72. Two important factors in the life of a gear are _____ and _____.

73. Gear teeth set too high will _____ teeth when carrying a load.

74. Gear teeth set too low will not properly _____.

75. Which of the following has the proper gear mesh. Figure _____.

FIGURE A   FIGURE B   FIGURE C

76. Indicate where the heel and toe are located on the drawing below:

B

A

GEAR TOOTH

77. Pattern is the _____ one gear leaves on the other when the teeth mesh.

78. The pattern must not be too close to the _____ or the _____ in order

   to distribute the load evenly on the gear.

79. The no _____ pattern often varies from the load pattern.

80. The _____ gear is stronger than the straight tooth gear of the same size.

81. The correct no load pattern for a spiral gear set would be figure _____.

TYPICAL ACCESSORY GEAR TOOTH PATTERN

ACCESSORY GEAR
(LOAD SIDE CONCAVED)

QUILL PINIONS
(LOAD SIDE CONVEX)

FIGURE A   FIGURE B   FIGURE C

82. Gear patterns can be _____ by moving gears in or out.

83. To control lash and patterns, gear packages are often used in conjunction with _____

_____.

84. Some newer gear boxes check _____ only.

85. If the lash is incorrect the gears must be _____ due to wear.

Chapter V
Main Rotor System

1. The main rotor system is exposed to many stresses during operation which include:

    a. _____

    b. _____

    c. _____

    d. _____ .

2. Each rotor system has certain _____ and _____ .

3. Today the most widely used rotors are the _____ and the _____

    _____ systems.

4. The rigid rotor system is used the _____ .

5. The two bladed rotor is known as the _____ rotor system.

6. Underslinging is normally associated with the _____ rotor system.

7. The rotor system utilizing the seesaw or _____ system is known as

    the semi-rigid rotor.

8. The feathering axis may also be referred to as the _____ axis.

9. The _____ rotor has provisions for independent blade flapping.

10. Lead and lag action is controlled by the use of a _____ .

11. Some rotor heads require _____ for lubrication while other use oil.

12. Most rotor heads are made of metal. However, one rotor head is now being built which uses_____

    _____ .

13. The basic member of the Bell 47 head is the _____ .

14. On the Bell 47 head, the _____ prevent fore and aft movement of the rotor blades.

15. The grip assemblies are held on the Bell 47 head by the use of thrust bearings and an _____.

16. The Bell 47 rotor system obtains underslinging by the use of a gimbal and _____ _____ arrangement.

17. The Hiller 12 rotor head utilizes _____ to hold the fork assemblies to the rotor head.

18. The _____ are used to change the pitch on the Hiller 12.

19. The Bell 206 rotor was originally designed for _____lubrication.

20. The yoke of the 206, like many other rotor systems, has a _____ angle built into the rotor.

21. The 206 uses tension torsion straps made of _____ rather than plates as is found in the Hiller 12.

22. The 206 blade retension bolts are hollow for the purpose of _____ balance.

23. The 206 utilizes a _____ mechanism rather than drag braces.

24. The S 58 rotor head has hinges for _____ and blade _____.

25. Thrust loads of the rotor head are carried by a stack of _____.

26. Flapping and droop on the S 58 are controlled by the _____ assembly.

27. The S 58 controls the rate of lead lag action by the use of _____ dampeners.

28. The Hughes 500 makes use of a _____ mast to support the rotor head.

29. The head of the Hughes 500 is supported by two _____ bearings.

30. The top and bottom sections of the head of the Hughes 500 are called the _____ assemblies.

31. The strap packs used in the Hughes 500 rotor carry:

   a. _____

   b. _____

   c. _____

32. The attachment of pendulums to the roots of the blades on the Hughes 500 C is for the purpose of dampening blade _____.

33. The 500 D is a _____ bladed rotor, while the 500 C is a _____ bladed rotor system.

34. The 500 C uses a _____ dampener, while the 500 D uses an _____ dampener to control lead lag of the rotor.

35. The S 76 has simplified the rotor head construction by the use of _____ bearings.

36. The S 76 uses a _____ vibration dampener.

37. The blade cuff and _____ are one piece on the S 76.

38. The lead lag, flap and pitch are furnished by an _____ bearing.

39. The "A" Star rotor head is made of _____.

40. No _____ life has been assigned to the components of the "A" Star head.

41. The "A" Star's flapping action is obtained by the _____ of the Star's arms.

42. The drag action on the "A" Star is accomplished by _____ of elastomerics.

43. The "A" Star's rotor makes use of a single weight installed in the top of the head as a _____ _____ dampening device.

44. The B0105 uses the only _____ rotor head in use today.

45. The B0105 rotor blades _____ to give the flap, lead lag action necessary.

ROTOR BLADES

46. Rotor blades may be made of:

    a. _____

    b. _____

    c. _____

47. The oldest type of rotor blade is the _____ blade.

48. In most instances, the wood is _____ of various types to form the blade.

49. A steel core installed in the wooden rotor blade acts as a _____.

50. The exterior of the wooden blade is covered with _____ cloth.

51. On the leading edge of the rotor blade is a stainless steel strip for _____.

52. The metal plates which are attached to the butt of the blade are commonly referred to as _____ _____.

53. The two tacks which are installed in the top of the wooden rotor blade denote the center of _____ _____ and the center of _____.

54. The _____ which is located at the outboard end of the blade is for the purpose of spanwise weight for balance.

55. Due to variations in the wood, the blades are used in matched _____.

56. Wooden rotor blades are affected by moisture which may cause a _____ problem.

57. No _____ life is assigned to wooden rotor blades.

58. The most serious damage can occur to the rotor when _____ because the impact is often transmitted to other parts of the blade.

59. When the rotor blade is repainted, it will be necessary to _____ the rotor system.

60. Wooden rotor blades may often be _____ when extensive repairs are required, rather than extended down time.

61. The _____ blade construction has limited the use of wooden blades.

62. One advantage of the metal blade is the ability to change _____ rather than matched sets.

63. Metal blades have a _____ life because of the stress placed on the blade.

64. Metal blades make use of bonded construction because of:

    a. _____

    b. _____

    c. _____

    d. _____

65. Metal blade construction is usually of _____ alloy.

66. Metal blades often make use of a spar which runs the entire _____ of the blade.

67. Weight is often added in the mid-span of the metal blade for _____.

68. _____ material is often used in blade construction in order to give shape and support to ths skin.

69. Grip plates and _____ are used at the butt of the blade to distribute the attachment stresses.

70. The _____ system is an electronic blade crack detection system used on some helicopter.

71. The _____ system utilizes an inert gas filled spar.

72. The BIM indicator will change _____ if a crack occurs in the spar.

73. Caustic cleaners should not be used on metal blades because of the adverse effect which they may have on the _____.

74. Nicks and scratches wil set up _____ in the metal blade.

75. Damage which is near the _____ of the blade is more critical than at the _____ portion of the blade.

76. Delamination of bonding and _____ sometimes occurs.

39

77. When metal rotor blades cannot be repaired in the field, _____ blades are often available from the manufacturer.

78. The newest material to be used in rotor blades is _____.

79. Some of the blades use a fiberglass spar while others use a _____ spar.

80. One advantage of the fiberglass blade is the apparent _____ of the blade with no time limitation.

81. The fiberglass blade is less susceptible to _____ damage than the metal blade.

ROTOR HEAD MAINTENANCE

82. Wet heads require less _____ servicing than heads which are greased.

83. The rotor head is a highly _____ unit and often contains many time change items.

84. The _____ contain a listing of items which require time changes.

85. Special inspections of the rotor system are required in the event of _____, sudden _____ and hard _____.

86. Some rotor heads may be removed with the rotor _____ installed while others will require _____ removal.

87. When removing a rotor head, the _____ is often locked by special holders in order to prevent damage during removal.

88. Torques required for rotor head installation is often quite high and may require a _____ _____ wrench.

89. Before attempting to remove a blade from the rotor head, it is important that the rotor blade be properly _____.

90. Some rotor blades are retained by bolts while others use taper _____.

91. Removed rotor blades should always be stored in _____ in order to prevent damage during storage.

92. Overhaul dimensions are quite often given in _____ of thousands, rather than thousandths of an inch.

93. During major inspections of the rotorhead, it is common practice to _____ all ferrous metal parts.

94. Manufacturers do not recommend replating of parts in the field because of hydrogen _____ _____.

95. The disposition of such items as hardware during overhaul is left to the _____ of the operator.

96. Color coding is often used on rotor head components for _____ purposes.

BLADE ALIGNMENT AND STATIC BALANCE

97. Blade alignment establishes the correct relationship of the center of _____ and the center of pressure.

98. Blade alignment is a required adjustment on _____ rotors.

99. Once the blade alignment is established, the blades may never be moved _____ of that point.

100. _____ points will be located on the rotor blades.

101. The blade _____ is often held in place during blade alignment by a fixture.

102. When the string method of blade alignment is used, _____ or squares may be used for sighting.

103. The movement of one drag brace will affect the _____ of both reference points.

104. Large, semi-rigid rotors often use the _____ method for blade alignment.

105. Blades that are properly aligned may need to be moved aft during _____ and dynamic balance.

106. Semi-rigid rotors will require _____ and _____ static balance.

107. _____ balance must be established prior to spanwise balance.

41

108. All static balancing should be accomplished in an area which is free from _____.

109. Wet heads should have all reservoirs _____ before static balancing.

110. Spanwise balance is obtained by adding weight:

a. _____

b. _____

111. Weights attached at other points by the manufacturer should not be _____ to obtain static balance.

112. On some rotor systems, chordwise balance is obtained by moving one blade _____ of the alignment point.

113. A universal balancer may be used for _____ and _____ of several helicopters with the use of adapters.

VIBRATION

114. Excessive _____ is the major contributor to component deterioration.

115. The cause of vibration is an _____ condition of rotating components.

116. Obtaining static balance does not insure _____ balance.

117. The movement of an unbalanced component is known as _____ or _____.

118. The rate at which a vibration occurs is known as _____.

119. The _____ and _____ determine if the vibration can be sensed by the human body.

120. Stationary components often vibrate because of the rotating component. This is known as a _____ vibration.

121. All rotating components have a _____ frequency of vibration.

122. To avoid continuous operation vibration range, a _____ range is often shown on the tachometer which is denoted by a red arc.

123. In helicopters, vibrations are classified into three groups which are:

   a. _____

   b. _____

   c. _____

124. _____ frequency vibration is at the rate of 0 to 500 rpm range.

125. **Probably, the easiest to detect and most common rotor vibration is the _____.**

126. Rotor vibration may either be _____ or _____ in nature.

127. _____ vibration is usually associated with track.

128. _____ vibration is usually associated with an imbalance condition of the rotor.

129. The 1:1 and 2:1 vibrations are easily _____ while multiple beats are not easy.

130. _____ frequency vibrations are in the 500 to 2000 rpm range.

131. _____ vibrations may be distinguishable as a beat to a buzz.

132. _____ vibrations are distinguishable as a buzz or tingling sensation.

133. Vibration will not only affect the life of the rotating components, but the life of _____ _____ components that vibrate in sympathy.

134. _____ often multiply rapidly as the component becomes older.

TRACKING

135. The rotor is in track when all rotor blades travel in the same _____.

136. The methods which may be used for tracking are:

   a. _____

   b. _____

   c. _____

   d. _____

   e. _____

137. All tracking begins with _____ tracking.

138. Many helicopters today also require _____ tracking as well.

139. No tracking may be accomplished under _____ conditions.

140. Using the stick method, indicate which blades in the following figures is in track and what corrective action is required on the other rotor.

_____

_____

_____

_____

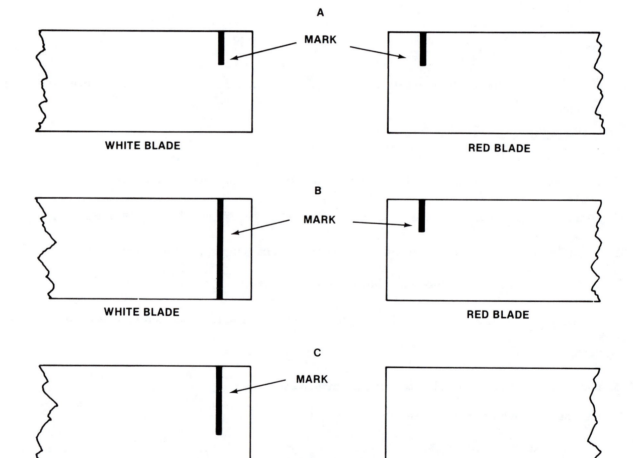

141. The flag and stick method of track may be used on _____ only.

142. Using the flag method, the coloring is applied to the _____.

143. Using the flag method of tracking, indicate which blades in the following figures is in track and the corrective action required in the remaining figures.

_____

_____

_____

_____

BLUE & RED (A)   RED BLUE (B)   BLUE RED (C)

144. The light reflector method may be used on the _____ and in the _____.

145. Using the light reflector method, which of the images represents the blades in track?

_____

_____

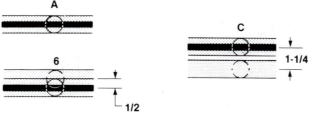

146. The _____ requires each blade to be flown against a

master blade when manufactured.

147. Using the system in the preceding question, the pitch change rod setting is given on the _____

_____ itself.

148. The electronic strobe system is similar to the _____ system except

that the images are superimposed.

149. Using the strobe system in the figures below, which set of images indicates that one blade is too high? What corrective action is required in the other figures?

_____

_____

_____

_____

_____

TIP PATH PLANE

(A)

(B)

(C)

150. The ground track is often adjusted by changing the _____ rods.

151. By changing the length of the rod, the _____ _____ of the blade is changed.

152. The use of _____ is usually limited to flight track changes.

153. In the following figure, which tab will make the blade fly higher?

_____

TAB

TAB

46

154. During initial tracking, the trim tabs should be placed in the _____ position.

155. If the tab is bent an excessive amount, the _____ will be disrupted, destroying the effect of the tab.

156. Blade crossover and a _____ are used to describe the same problem.

157. The problem of climbing blades occurs when the helicopter is in forward _____.

158. The cause of a climbing blade is that of one blade being more _____ than the other blade.

159. A _____ track may be used to determine the high blade in flight.

160. When tracking, in the preceding question, the _____ blade is the _____ blade in flight.

161. No dynamic balance should be attempted until the _____ has been properly adjusted.

DYNAMIC BALANCING

162. When no electronic balancing equipment is available, the dynamic balancing is a _____ _____ system.

163. _____ one blade to see if the vibration lowered is used for spanwise balance.

164. When the vibration level is reduced to acceptable standards, the weight of the _____ must be added to the _____.

165. This method of _____ greatly depends upon the sensitivity of the maintenance technician to feel the vibration.

166. In addition to spanwise balance, it is possible to have _____ balance problems on semi rigid rotors.

167. It is not unusual to have _____ and _____ imbalance at the same time.

47

168. One _____ often masks the other until one is removed.

169. _____ dynamic balance is obtained by sweeping one blade.

170. If the amplitude of the vibration remains constant throughout the rpm range, it is said to be out of _____ balance.

171. Other indications of the problem of chordwise balance are _____ collective and _____ of the cyclic.

172. When sweeping rotor blades, all movements must be made in the _____ direction only.

173. When sweeping blades, a small movement of the drag brace is multiplied several times at the _____ _____ tip.

174. Shortening the drag brace moves the blade _____.

ELECTRONIC BALANCING

175. One of the latest developments in vibration analysis is the _____.

176. Vibration is sensed through an _____ when using this equipment.

177. A _____ is used in order to eliminate all vibrations other than those which are sought.

178. The vibration meter measures vibration in _____ _____ of amplitude.

179. It is easily possible to reduce the vibration level to less than _____ IPS.

180. Interrupters and a _____ are attached at the swashplate in order to determine the postition of the vibration in the rotor system.

181. This system is the triggering portion of the _____ which will be used with a graph in order to determine the corrective action.

182. The chart is _____ for each helicopter type.

183. Using the chart for semi rigid rotors, corrections may be made for both _____ imbalance and _____ imbalance.

184. On the chart below, determine what corrective action should be taken:

_____

_____

_____

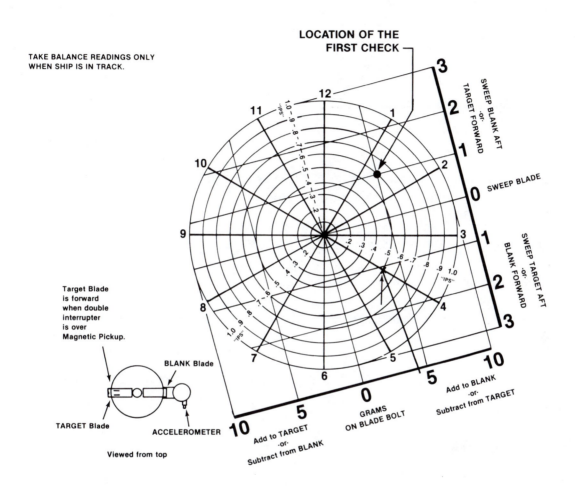

185. Corrections on fully articulated rotors may be made only for _____

imbalance.

186. If the first move on the chart increases the vibration level, it may be necessary to use the _____

_____.

DAMPENERS

187. Most fully articulated rotors use dampeners to control movement about the _____

_____ axis of the rotor blades.

188. The three basic types of dampeners in use today are the:

    a. _____

    b. _____

    c. _____

189. A faulty dampener will cause an_____ condition of the rotor by the blade seeking the wrong position.

190. The _____ dampener controls the lead lag movement by an orifice which restricts the flow of fluid.

191. The _____ dampener has a rotating and stationary disk.

192. The _____ dampener is the only type which requires the blades to be aligned.

193. One bad dampener would result in a _____ beat or scuffle.

194. Often the condition of the dampener may be determined by _____

_____

_____

195. A _____ may be used to observe the blade phasing while the helicopter is operating.

COLLECTIVE ADJUSTMENT

196. Some helicopters make use of _____ to aid in raising the collective.

197. Too _____ of a collective would require additional weight to be added.

198. The correctly adjusted collective should remain in the _____ position "hands off".

AUTOROTATION

199. When adjustments are made to the main rotor, the _____ characteristics may be affected.

200. If the autorotation speed is too fast _____ may occur.

201. If the autorotation speed is too slow, the_____ will not

support the helicopter.

202. The autorotation rpm is affected by:

a. _____

b. _____

203. Autorotation adjustments are made by _____

_____ .

Chapter VI
Mast And Flight Controls

1. The mast usually absorbs _____ and _____ loads.

2. The mast is a critical item and sometimes has a _____ life assigned to it.

3. The mast is used to support the rotor head and on some helicopters, it is also used to support the _____ assembly.

4. The mast on the Bell 47 is equipped with five sets of splines which are used for:

   a. _____

   b. _____

   c. _____

   d. _____

   e. _____

5. The mast on the Hughes "500" is a _____ mast.

6. The use of this type of mast requires the use of a _____ in addition to the mast.

7. The Hughes "500" mast is stressed for _____ and _____ loads only.

8. The drive shaft is splined to the _____ and bolted to the rotor head.

9. The rotor is supported by the mast by two tapered _____ bearings and locked by a locknut.

10. Masts used on other helicopters sometimes include such features as _____ passing through the center of the mast.

11. Scratches on the mast are critical. They may sometimes be _____ in accordance with manufacturer's recommendations.

12. Mast damage which is due to mast bump is associated with _____ rotor systems.

13. At overhaul the mast is checked:

    a. _____

    b. _____

    c. _____

14. Several models of Bell Helicopters utilize a _____ system.

15. The stabilizer bar utilizes the principle of gyroscopic _____ for their operation.

16. The stabilizer will remain in its plane of _____ when the rotor is disturbed by an outside force.

17. Movement of the stabilizer bar is controlled at a predetermined rate by the _____ _____.

18. The _____ is a safety device in the event that the outer tube breaks.

19. The stabilizer bar requires _____ balance in order to insure a smooth operation.

20. The dampeners on the Bell _____ are adjustable, whereas those used on other models are not adjustable.

21. Soft and hard spots may often be felt by raising and lowering the _____ by hand.

22. A dampener which is too soft will result in an overstable helicopter with _____ control response.

23. A dampener which is too hard will result in an unstable helicopter with too _____ of a control response.

24. The swashplate transfers _____ and _____ control movements from a stationary movement to a rotating movement.

25. When collective is applied, all rotor blades must change _____ at the same time.

26. The collective control requires an up and down movement of the _____.

27. Cyclic control movements require the rotor to tilt:

    a. _____

    b. _____

    c. _____

    d. _____

28. This cyclic movement requires a universal joint movement in the _____.

29. For cyclic movement to take place, the non-rotating part of the swashplate moves in the _____ _____ direction as the desired rotor movement. However, the rotating portion must apply the force _____ in the same direction as rotation.

30. This directional input from the swashplate to the rotor is due to gyroscopic _____ _____.

31. During many maneuvers, both inputs are applied to the _____ in conjunction with each other.

32. The rotating part of the swashplate is driven by a drive link which is attached to the _____ _____ assembly on most helicopters.

33. One of the most important steps in the maintenance of the swashplate is to keep the moveable surfaces _____.

34. Checking the tension on the uniball of the 206 is accomplished with the use of a spring _____ _____.

35. Hydraulic _____ is often required on large helicopters for control movement.

36. The collective control is usually located on the _____ side of the pilot.

37. The _____ control movement is up and down.

38. On reciprocating engine helicopters, the collective has a _____ which controls the throttle.

39. The collective twist grip on free turbine helicopters is used to control _____

rpm and to operate the helicopter engine in the emergency mode.

40. The switch box located on the top of some collectives may contain:

a. _____

b. _____

c. _____

41. The collective usually has a _____ adjustment.

42. The collective should not be so heavy as to creepdown or so light that it moves _____

_____.

43. The cyclic control is used to tilt the rotor in _____ directions.

44. Switches added to the cyclic control grip may include:

a. _____

b. _____

45. The friction for the cylic is usually located at the _____ of the control.

46. _____ tubes are commonly used in collective and cyclic control systems.

47. These tubes often use _____ or _____ rod ends.

48. Some rod ends are _____ while other ends are fixed.

49. Since the tubes are hollow, they are often _____ _____ with Pro Seal or Metal Set.

50. Some rod ends are riveted into place which usually requires _____ rivets.

51. Threaded rod ends are often replaced to the same length by counting the threads or the use of a

_____.

52. Most push-pull tubes require _____ bolts for connection.

53. It is not unusual to find _____ castle nuts on control tubes.

54. Torque tubes may be used to convert _____ motion into _____ motion.

55. Bell cranks may be used to:

a. _____

b. _____

56. One device using bell cranks and torque tubes, is the _____.

57. The purpose of the mixer is to prevent _____ input from affecting _____ input.

58. The gradient is basically a _____ unit.

59. The gradient spring is _____ by control movement in either direction.

60. Gradients may be found on the following controls:

    a. _____

    b. _____

    c. _____

61. Gradients are installed in conjunction with flight controls but never as an _____ part of the system.

62. When gradients are used in conjunction with _____ they assist in trimming the helicopter.

63. In trimming the helicopter, the cyclic is moved the required distance for the ship to be level and the _____ is applied.

64. The force used to keep the helicopter in trim is the _____ spring pressure.

65. Other helicopters which do not use magnetic brakes sometime use _____ motors for trimming the helicopter.

66. The trim motor simply sets tension on a _____ installed in the control system.

67. Helicopters not utilizing hydraulic boost for controls often use:

    a. _____

    b. _____

    c. _____

68. Hydraulic boost systems found in most light helicopters are for _____ the pilot in the control of the helicopter.

69. Large helicopters often require hydraulic boost to _____ the helicopter in flight. These aircraft often have dual boost systems.

70. The hydraulic boost system usually has the pump driven from the _____

_____.

71. The reservoirs for these systems are usually equipped with a sight _____ for

checking fluid levels.

72. The pressure used for hydraulic boost may be as low as 250 psi or a high as _____ psi.

73. Many of the newer filtering systems have warning _____ to indicate when

the filter is bypassing.

74. The filters used in these boost systems are either of a _____ type

or may require ultrasonic cleaning.

75. If accumulators are used in the boost system, they are usually of the conventional _____

_____ type.

76. Some hydraulic actuators move the piston, while others move the _____.

77. All of these actuators are equipped with pilot and _____ valves.

78. Dual actuators are fed by _____ separate hydraulic systems.

79. Movement of the cyclic moves the pilot valve or _____ valve.

80. The movement of the servo valve directs fluid to one side of the cylinder and _____

of the other side of the cylinder.

81. When the valve port closes fluid is _____ inside the cylinder.

82. If hydraulic pressure is lost, all fluid is trapped inside the cylinder. This forms a closed circuit for

_____ movement.

83. Feedback from the rotor system is often hidden from the control _____ system.

84. In one unit, the Jet Ranger has a reservoir, _____ and relief valve.

85. The Bell 206 system has a _____ valve which is used to turn off hydraulic boost.

86. This valve routes the fluid back to the _____.

87. The valve is _____ when the system is off.

88. The Bell 206 has three servos on most models. One of these is operated by the collective and the other two are operated by the _____ control.

89. The Bell 212 utilizes a _____ hydraulic boost system.

90. The Bell 212 system operates hydraulic boost on the following controls:

a. _____

b. _____

c. _____

91. On the Bell 212, one portion of the hydraulic boost operates the _____. All other controls are operated by both systems.

92. The Bell 212 has fluid from Systems 1 and Systems 2 routed to dual actuators. Fluid from System 1 is routed to the _____ of the actuator and System 2 goes to the _____ of the actuator.

93. Fluid from the two systems _____ contact each other in the system.

94. The Bell 212 system uses _____ pumps.

95. The Bell 212 system operates on a maximum pressure of _____ psi.

96. Two filters are installed in the Bell 212 system, one is a _____ filter and one is a _____ filter.

97. One of the filters in the 212 system has a bypass which is the _____ filter.

98. The Bell 212 has provisions for shutting off either system in case of malfunction. This is done by the use of a _____ valve.

99. The 212 dual actuators are equipped on the top and bottom with a _____ and a _____ valve.

100. The upper servo valve directs fluid to the upper or lower side of the _____ with the cylinder remaining stationary.

101. The lower servo valve directs fluid to the lower piston and moves the _____.

102. On the Bell 212 system, either servo may be moved if the other is jammed by the use of _____ _____.

103. If System 1 is not functioning, the upper piston is moved by the _____.

104. If System 2 is not functioning, the lower cylinder is moved by the _____.

105. When both systems are inoperative, seal leakage is replenished by the _____.

106. With both systems inoperative the actuators will remain _____ as long as fluid remains in the system.

107. High usage of fluid is an indication of _____.

108. When filters are changed the system must be checked under _____ for filter leaks.

109. It is common practice to inspect hydraulic systems using an _____ pressure system.

110. Maintenance of hydraulic components in the field are usually limited to _____ and _____.

111. Replacement of excessive numbers of rod ends is usually an indication of excessive rotor _____ _____.

112. After the initial rigging of a helicopter is completed, minor _____ are often required after the flight test.

113. The use of rigging _____ and rigging _____ have simplified the task of rigging controls.

114. On most helicopters, the cyclic control system is rigged with the cyclic stick in the _____ _____ position.

115. When rigging the cyclic, the hydraulic servo valves are usually placed in a neutral _____. _____.

116. Extreme positions of the swashplate are often set by mechanical _____.

117. Most helicopters have interconnections between the collective and cyclic systems such as the Bell 206. This requires positioning both the _____ and _____ _____ before either system is rigged.

118. The cyclic of the Bell 206 is positioned by placing a _____ through the cabin floor.

119. On the Bell 206, all controls must be checked for clearances before _____ power is applied after rigging.

120. The "A" Star 350 uses _____ pins in both the collective and cyclic control systems.

121. The "A" Star 350 swashplate is held in place by a rigging _____ during rigging operation.

122. During basic control rigging, items such as _____ and magnetic brakes are disconnected from the system.

123. Moveable elevators are sometimes connected to the _____ control system.

124. The moveable elevator increases the controlability and the _____ of the helicopter.

Chapter VII
Main Rotor Transmissions

1. Main rotors turn at speeds of _____ to _____ hundred rpm on most helicopters.

2. A reciprocating powerplant often operates at _____ rpm when installed in helicopters.

3. Turbine engines mounted in helicopters may operate at _____ output shaft rpm.

4. Rotors cannot operate at engine rpm because of rotor _____ speed and retreating _____ stall.

5. Engines produce their greatest amount of power at _____ rpm.

6. Transmissions are used to _____ engine speed in order to be compatible with rotor speeds.

7. The location of the _____ is quite important to the basic design of the transmission.

8. Most of the early light helicopters had reciprocating engines mounted _____ coupled to the transmission.

9. Some of the early heavy helicopters had engines mounted in the _____ driving the transmission by shafting.

10. Two different reciprocating powered helicopters manufactured today have the engines mounted _____ driving the transmission by belts.

11. The Bell 47 has the engine attached to the transmission by the use of an _____ plate.

12. One belt driven system utilizes eight V-belts which are driven from a _____ pulley attached to the engine.

13. A drive shaft system is used on some helicopters between the engine and the _____ _____. When drive shafts are used, they often incorporate a clutch with the drive shaft.

14. Most turbine powered helicopters make use of a _____ to connect the engine to the transmission.

15. The short shaft must have a method to correct for _____ between the engine and transmission.

16. Many of the shortshafts require lubrication in the form of hand packed _____.

17. The Bell 206 driveshaft has two _____ attached at each end of the shaft.

18. Flexibility is obtained by the use of _____that ride on the splines of the outer coupling.

19. The Bell 206 shaft is centered by the use of _____.

20. The Hughes 500's short shaft is made in three sections and are welded at the flanges by an _____ _____ welding process.

21. No _____ is required on the Hughes 500's shaft because of the three piece flexible joints.

22. The drive shaft used on the "A" Star is enclosed in a _____.

23. The purpose of the housing is to absorb _____ or compression loads.

24. The "A" Star drive shaft couplings are made up of _____ stacked together to form a flexible joint.

25. The Bell 47's drive gear will require _____and a tooth wear check at major inspection periods.

26. Helicopters that use belt drives usually have a _____ life assigned to the belts.

27. The Hiller 12E has a steel and rubber bonded coupling which must be checked for:

   a. _____

   b. _____

   c. _____

28. Failure of grease seals on short shafts can lead to _____ of the shaft due to loss of grease.

29. Some drive shafts require alignment of the _____ and _____ _____.

30. Clutch units are found in helicopters powered by _____ engines and those not using _____ turbines.

31. The clutch is necessary to unload the engine during _____ because of the forces required to move the rotor.

32. The clutch unit is always located between the _____ and the _____ _____.

33. The clutch may be engaged _____ or _____ depending upon the design.

34. The free wheeling unit is sometimes referred to as the _____.

35. All helicopters are equipped with a free _____.

36. On multi engine helicopters, one free wheeling unit is present for each _____.

37. The free wheeling unit allows the engine to drive the _____ but prevents the _____ from driving the engine.

38. Without the free wheeling unit, _____ would not be possible.

39. The operation of the free wheeling unit is always _____.

40. The Bell 47's clutch is a _____ clutch which operates automatically.

41. The shoes of the Bell 47 clutch are driven from the _____.

42. The Bell 47 clutch drum is attached to the _____.

65

43. The Hiller 12 clutch is commonly referred to as a _____ clutch.

44. The drum of the Hiller clutch is cooled by _____.

45. Oil leakage on the shoes of the Hiller clutch will cause _____.

46. The Bell 47's clutch is cooled by _____.

47. The clutch used on the Gazelle is a centrifugal _____ clutch.

48. The forward portion of the Gazelle clutch is attached to the _____

shaft.

49. The Gazelle clutch engages when the engine rpm reaches _____ to 33,000 rpm.

50. Helicopters utilizing belt drives use a _____ as a clutch.

51. These clutch systems require engagement by the _____.

52. In one belt system the clutch is engaged by the use of a _____.

53. Disengagement of this type of clutch at high rpm could result in an _____.

54. Some reciprocating powered helicopters use a _____.

55. Engagement of this type of clutch is always smooth because of the _____ coupling.

56. The clutch pump utilizes _____for fluid.

57. The fluid coupling consists of a driving member and a _____ member.

58. In this hydro mechanical clutch, the _____ unit makes a

mechanical coupling when rotor rpm is obtained.

59. Some of the older helicopters have the free wheeling unit built into the _____.

60. Many helicopters have the free wheeling unit located in the _____ of the engine.

61. Regardless of the location of the free wheeling unit, the tail rotor must rotate during _____

_____.

62. The _____ unit is the most common free wheeling unit in use.

63. The sprag unit allows movement to be transmitted in only _____ direction.

64. The sprag unit is made up of:

a. _____

b. _____

c. _____

65. The sprags are shaped like a figure _____.

66. The vertical height of the sprag is slightly _____ than the gap between the outer and inner races.

67. The sprags are held in the _____ position by a spring loaded cage.

68. When the _____ race is driven by the engine, the sprags jam against the _____ race making a solid connection.

69. If the rotor attempts to drive the engine, the _____ release and the rotor turns freely without the engine.

70. Belt driven helicopters utilize a sprag unit in the belt _____.

71. The Bell 206 sprag system is installed at the engine _____ end.

72. During autorotation, the main rotor of the Bell 206 drives the:

a. _____

b. _____

73. The oil for lubrication of the sprag unit is supplied by the _____.

74. The sprag unit of the Hughes 500 is mounted on the _____ of the engine output shaft.

75. The sprag unit of the Hughes 500 is attached to the engine output shaft by _____.

76. The Hughes 500's sprag unit bearings are handpacked with _____ for lubrication.

77. The sprags of the Hughes 500 are lubricated by _____.

78. A roller type free wheeling unit is used on the Aerospatiale's _____.

79. In this unit the rollers are trapped between a _____ shaft and the free wheeling head.

80. In normal operation, the rollers make contact with the _____ side and wedge the rollers to the _____ forming a solid unit.

81. When autorotation occurs, the rollers change position and make contact with the lobe _____ _____ seperating the two shafts.

82. Torquemeters are located on all _____ powered helicopters.

83. Most torquemeters are located within the _____ engine.

84. The Aerospatiale Gazelle has the torquemeter located between the _____ and _____.

85. The torquemeter is used to measure _____ of the turbine engine.

86. Engine power is sometimes limited because of the _____.

87. The torquemeter on the Gazelle is an _____ detection device.

88. This device measures the angular _____ _____ between two discs.

89. The discs are attached to the two ends of the _____ between the engine and transmission.

90. This device measures the amount of _____ in the power shaft.

91. The two discs are surrounded by the torque _____ _____.

92. A light beam passes through a window in one of the _____.

93. The amount of light passing through the window is dependent upon the position of the other _____.

94. The torquemeter indicator gives a readout in _____ of torque.

95. Some helicopters have a _____ located between the engine and the transmission.

96. This component is used to stop the rotor after engine _____.

97. Without the rotor brake, the _____ of the main rotor will continue to move the main rotor after engine shutdown.

68

98. Most operators limit the use of the rotor brake because of the _____ of the brake unit.

99. Brake units are normally attached to the input to the _____.

100. The brake may be either _____ or _____ operated.

101. The unit used on the Bell 206 is _____.

102. The master cylinder for this unit is installed on the _____.

103. The brake unit is a singular disc _____ brake pad system.

104. The brake system _____ utilize the hydraulic system of the helicopter.

105. The "A" Star 350 utilizes a _____ operated rotor brake system.

106. This brake unit uses a _____ housing and a _____ housing.

107. Between the fixed and moveable housing is a _____. This keeps the moveable housing off the disc when the brake is not _____.

108. The brake is actuated by a control _____.

109. To inspect the clutch, the engine is run and the _____ needles are checked for engagement.

110. During all normal operations, the two needles of the _____ should stay superimposed.

111. During starting, the _____ rpm will be ahead of the _____ rpm until the clutch is fully engaged.

112. If the free wheeling unit is inoperative, the helicopter would have problems with _____ _____.

113. The free wheeling unit is checked during pre-flight run up with the use of the _____ _____.

114. When power is reduced rapidly, the two needles of the tachometer should _____.

115. A slipping clutch on the Bell 47 may indicate the need to change the _____ lining.

116. The Hiller 12's clutch may slip due to a low _____ level in the clutch.

69

117. Some free wheeling units carry their own _____ which requires servicing.

118. Periodic inspections of all sprag units is required because of the _____ factors of the units.

119. Transmissions are usually mounted of semi-flexible mounts in order to dampen _____

_____.

120. Rotor vibrations are _____ and _____ by loads placed on the rotor in flight.

121. These vibrations can start _____ and _____ vibrations in the fuselage.

122. In addition to the requirement of the mount to have flexibility, it must also carry the weight of the helicopter and absorb the _____ loads of the rotor system.

123. The Bell 47 transmission mount is also the _____ mount.

124. The Bell 47 mount system consists of:

a. _____

b. _____

c. _____

d. _____

125. The _____ is bolted to the engine and suspended by two trunnion pins.

126. The trunnion pins give the _____ and _____ flexibility from side to side.

127. The basket is attached to the center of the helicopter through two rubber._____

_____.

128. The Bell 47 has a _____ system placed on the bottom of the engine.

129. This system offers both _____ and _____ to the movement of the engine and transmission unit.

70

130. In case of sprag mount failure, the engine transmission unit travel is limited by a _____ _____ system.

131. The engine mount on the Bell 47 has a _____ life due to the stresses imposed.

132. All rubber mounts used on the Bell 47 are inspected for general _____ throughout their life.

133. The threaded rod ends of the sprag mount are used to align the _____.

134. Incorrect adjustment of the sprag system can affect the _____ characteristics and cause abnormal _____.

135. The transmission of the Bell 206 is mounted seperately of the _____.

136. The Bell 206 transmission is mounted to the cabin roof by two _____ on each side of the transmission.

137. The fore and aft movement of the transmission is restricted by the _____.

138. This mount is made up of layers of _____ and metal bonded together.

139. The mount returns the mast and transmission to its _____ position whenever it is displaced by rotor loads.

140. The spike and hole arrangement on the bottom of the Bell 206 transmission is a _____ _____ device in the case of the isolation mount failing.

141. The shims under the pylon mounts are for the purpose of engine to transmission _____ _____.

142. The nodal beam system is used to dampen the _____ vibration normally associated with semi rigid rotors.

143. The transmission, mast and rotor are isolated from the _____ by the nodal beam.

144. The _____ assemblies are the primary vibration absorbing unit of the nodal beam system.

145. These assemblies are provided with _____ weights for tuning the beam.

146. The Bell 206L nodal beam system also uses a transmission restraint to limit _____ and _____ movement of the transmission.

147. The _____ link is used as means of transferring rotor loads to the airframe during flight.

148. The transmission of the Hughes 500 carries _____ rotor loads during flight.

149. To obtain high strength to weight ratios, the preferred gears for transmissions are _____ _____ and _____ gears for directional changes.

150. Some helicopter transmissions utilize _____ gear reduction systems.

151. In addition to supplying power for the main rotor, the Bell 47 transmission supplies power to the:

    a. _____

    b. _____

    c. _____

    d. _____

    e. _____

152. The Bell 47 transmission receives oil for lubrication from the _____.

153. The rotor tachometer drive is located at the _____ with the main rotor mast support.

154. The four accessory drives are located around the _____ case.

155. The Bell 47 transmission may be broken into major subassemblies. These are:

    a. _____

    b. _____

    c. _____

    d. _____

156. The Bell 47's clutch operates in _____ and is of a centrifugal type.

157. The clutch shoes are pinned to the _____ which is splined to the crankshaft adapter gear.

158. When the Bell 47 clutch is fully engaged, the _____ and the spider turn as a unit.

159. The clutch drum is splined to the lower _____.

160. The lower case is aluminum with steel liners for the following:

a. _____

b. _____

c. _____

d. _____

e. _____

161. The lower sun passes through the lower case _____.

162. The lower case bearing is a _____ piece roller bearing that supports the lower sun gear.

163. The upper teeth of the lower sun gear mesh with the teeth of the _____ of the lower planetary gear.

164. The accessory drive gear is supported by _____ angular contact bearing.

165. The lower plantetary spider splines on the top and bottom. The top splines drive the upper _____ _____. The bottom splines fit over the _____ drive gear.

166. The lower spider holds eight _____ gear.

167. Surrounding the lower planetary is the _____ unit.

168. The inner ring of the wheeling unit acts as a _____ while the engine is driving the rotor.

169. When the rotor is driving, the inner ring acts as a _____.

170. The outer ring of the free wheeling unit provides a rolling surface in _____ and _____ surface during engine engagement.

171. _____ and _____ assemblies are located between the inner and outer rings.

172. The free wheeling unit locks in the _____ direction.

173. The **upper sun gear** is splined to the top of the lower spider and meshes with the upper spider _____

    _____.

174. The **upper spider** is splined to drive the _____.

175. Transmissions built today _____ the engine oil system from the transmission

    oil system.

176. _____ temperature is always a good indicator of the condition of the transmission.

177. The Bell 47 transmission has shims on each quill which determine the gear _____

    and _____.

178. The condition of the clutch shoes of the Bell 47 are checked at _____ intervals.

179. Wear on gear teeth are usually checked with the use of _____.

180. The Bell 206 transmission has no clutch nor does it have an internal _____

    _____ unit as does the Bell 47.

181. The transmission case of the Bell 206 is made up of two pieces: the _____ and

    the top case.

182. The main case provides a housing for the:

    a. _____

    b. _____

    c. _____

    d. _____

183. The input quill transmists engine power to the _____.

184. The pinion hear is supported by a set of _____ bearings.

185. The pinion gear meshes with the _____ gear.

186. The sun gear is splined to the inside of the main _____ and drives the

    planetary pinions.

187. The planetary pinions walk around a _____ gear mounted in the uppercase.

188. The center of the carrier is splined to accommodate the _____.

189. The Bell 206 has _____ accessory drive quill.

190. The accessory drive is driven by the _____ gear.

191. The accessory drive gear turns the following:

    a. _____

    b. _____

    c. _____

192. The oil system lubricates the transmission and the _____ unit.

193. The oil pump used in the Bell 206 is a _____ type pump.

194. The oil filter head is mounted to the outside of the _____ .

195. The filter head provides an attachment for the filter and incorporates:

    a. _____ _____

    b. _____

196. The oil cooler is cooled by a fan driven by the _____ shaft.

197. The oil _____ omit the cooler during starting and cold weather.

198. Two oil jets are located on the _____ and _____

    _____ case.

199. The oil level of the Bell 206 transmission is checked by a _____ on the lower

    case.

200. The accessory drive gear and the input drive gear require a _____ check only at

    major inspections when installed.

201. The Hughes 500 transmission is located below the _____ mast.

202. Access to the transmission is gained from inside the _____ .

203. No _____ unit or _____ are located in the

    Hughes 500's transmission.

204. Power input is made through a _____ shaft.

205. The power input is placed on the same angle as the _____ .

206. The input pinion gear engages the _____ output pinion gear.

207. Attached with the tail rotor drive gear is the _____ gear.

208. The _____ gear reduces the rpm to 485.

209. All of the main gears in the Hughes 500 transmission are _____ gears.

210. Two accessory pads are located on the _____ and _____ side of the tail rotor output shaft.

211. The accessory pads are driven from a _____ gear pinned to the tail rotor output shaft.

212. The two accessory pads drive the:

    a. _____

    b. _____

    c. _____

213. The lubrication system of the Hughes 500 transmission utilizes the following operations:

    a. _____

    b. _____

    c. _____

    d. _____

    e. _____

    f. _____

    g. _____

214. The Hughes 500 transmission uses an externally mounted _____ pressure pump.

215. Oil from the pressure pump goes to the _____.

216. Oil bypasses the oil cooler when the _____ is too low.

217. The oil coller blower is powered by the _____.

218. The oil filter is a _____ filter.

219. The scavenge pump oil is used to lubricate the upper cylinder bearings of the _____.

Chapter VIII
Powerplants

1. Helicopters which are powered by reciprocating engines use engines which were once used on _____ _____ aircraft.

2. Many of the helicopter reciprocating engines were mounted _____ rather than horizontally.

3. Modifications were required to some of the systems such as the _____ system because of the repositioning of the engines.

4. The engine installed in a helicopter is required to operate at a _____ rpm than a fixed wing aircraft.

5. Increasing the maximum speed is one method of increasing the _____.

6. All reciprocating engines require a _____ for cooling.

7. Main rotors usually operate at a _____ rpm.

8. On helicopter installations, the engine power is controlled in order to maintain the _____ rpm.

9. _____ rpm for idle is required on helicopter installations.

10. Reciprocating engines on helicopters use carburetor heat more frequently than fixed wing aircraft because of the lack of _____ action.

11. The establishment of transient rpm ranges is due to the _____ of the airframe system.

12. Early Bell 47 and Hillers use _____ opposed engines; later models use _____ engines.

13. Some of the engines used in the Bells and Hillers became _____ engines with a separate oil tank.

14. Oil coolers were added to most of these engines which received cooling air from the _____ _____.

15. Some of the early engines were mounted vertically and backward which changed the location of the _____.

16. _____ and compression tests became move difficult because the crankshaft was mounted directly to the clutch and transmission.

17. Some opposed engines were equipped with a _____ to aid in turning the engine by hand.

18. Some of the larger, early helicopters used _____ engines rather than opposed engines.

19. Most of these engines were located in the _____ of the helicopter.

20. The output shafts of the engines faced _____ and _____ toward the transmission.

21. Two of the newer, opposed engine helicopters have the engine mounted in the _____ _____ position in the middle of the fuselage.

22. All reciprocating engines mounted in helicopters require a cooling system because they receive no cooling from _____ as the fixed wing aircraft.

23. The Bell 47 has a fan mounted on the _____ of the engine.

24. The Bell 47 fan is powered by a matched set of _____.

25. This fan turns at a _____ speed than the engine.

26. The belts are driven from the _____ mounted on the transmission.

27. The double pulley located on the fan is _____ than the transmission pulley.

28. The belt tension is adjusted on the _____ assembly.

29. The Hiller cooling fan is driven by a _____ and _____ rather than a belt system.

30. The cooling fan shroud on the Hiller 12 is made of either _____ or

_____ depending on the model.

31. Cracks in the cooling fans usually occur at the _____ of the blade.

32. These cracks often occur from operating in a _____ rpm range.

33. Fans are usually _____ balanced prior to installtion.

34. Vibration from the cooling fans is usually felt as a _____ because of the high

frequency.

35. A twist grip on the _____ is used for throttle operation on reciprocating engine.

36. This twist grip is similar to those used on motorcylces except the action is in the _____

_____ direction.

37. The decrease position of the twist grip is towards the _____ as the hand grips the

collective.

38. The _____ box eliminates the need of adding throttle as the collective is

raised and lowered.

39. On the Bell 47 the throttle is moved by the _____ or the twist grip.

40. The _____ transforms the push-pull movement to a rotary movement for

throttle movement.

41. The cam is necessary because the _____ output is not a straight

line movement.

42. The cam actually establishes the correct _____ for the blade pitch.

43. The cam is actually an irregular _____ cut in the metal with a follower.

44. Replacement of the _____ will require rerigging the correlation system.

45. Collective rigging will _____ the correlation rigging.

46. The fine adjustments are made to the _____ after the test flight.

47. The turbine engines were the first engines designed specifically for _____

_____ installation.

48. The turbines used in helicopters range in power from _____ to _____ horsepower.

49. The turbines used in helicopters are referred to as shaft turbines or _____ engines.

50. The shaft turbine is designed to produce _____ rather than thrust.

51. The turboshaft engines usually contain a _____ to reduce turbine speed.

52. Turboshaft engines are further classified as _____ turbines or _____ turbines.

53. The most popular of these turbines for helicopter installation is the _____ turbine.

54. The free turbine delivers power from a turbine not connected to the _____.

55. The direct drive turbine engine turns at the same speed as the _____ because they share a common shaft.

56. The free turbine varies the speed of the compressor to meet the demands of the _____ _____ power.

57. Most of the helicopter turbines, today, use a compressor which is a combination of _____ _____ and _____ compressors.

58. The first portion of the compressor will be _____ and the last stage is centrifugal.

59. By reducing the number of axial stages with the centrifugal compressor, the length of the engine is _____.

60. The speed of the airflow is _____ by using the combination of the axial and centrifugal compressor.

61. Each stage of the axial compressor is made up of one _____ and one _____.

62. The rotor _____ the velocity of the airflow and the stator develops the

_____.

63. The centrifugal compressor has a _____ inlet than outlet.

64. Air entering the combustor is used to support _____ and cooling purposes.

65. The most common combustor used on turboshafts, is the _____ combustor.

66. Many of the turbines use a combustor which has _____ flow of the air.

67. The air entering the combustor is mixed with fuel and ignited which _____

the air.

68. These gasses pass through a _____ upon leaving the combustor.

69. A turbine engine turns a _____ turbine wheel with the expanded gasses.

70. The free turbine has a least one turbine wheel after the compressor turbine to drive a _____

_____ which powers the helicopter.

71. Turbine engines may drive from the _____ end or the _____ end

depending upon the manufacturer.

72. Many of today's turboshaft engines produce more than a _____ per

pound weight.

73. Turboshaft horsepower is usually expressed in _____.

74. Thrust produced by the turboshaft engine is of little _____ in helicopter

operation.

75. Flat rated engines are capable of producing maximum power at temperatures in _____

of standard day values.

76. Torque limited is a term used in relation to the _____ that may be delivered

to the transmission.

77. The helicopter engine only produces the power _____ by the helicopter

operator in various flight modes.

78. The _____ of the rotor blades determines the power required to maintain a

constant rpm.

81

79. Power is measured by the _____ pressure gauge on reciprocating engines.

80. The power output of turbine engines is measured by a _____ on turboshaft engines.

81. The most convienent measurement of torque is in the form of _____.

82. Both the _____ and _____ are the determining factors of engine power.

83. On free turbines, two tachometers are used: one reads _____ speed and the other reads _____ speed.

84. The tachometers used on turboshaft engines often reads in _____ of maximum rpm because of turbine speed.

85. The N_2 tachometer usually is a dual tachometer showing _____ and _____ speed.

86. Free turbines often operate with different readings on the _____ and _____ tachometers.

87. During ground operation, the compressor tachometer will read _____ than the power turbine tachometer.

88. Droop occurs when the N_2 rpm _____ when the collective is raised.

89. The Egt guage measures the temperature of the _____.

90. The Egt guage is carefully monitored during _____ and takeoffs with heavy loads and high ambient temperatures.

91. Warm up periods for turbine engines are _____ as crititical as reciprocating engines in regards to lubrication.

92. Most helicopters require a _____ on the inlet of the turbine engine.

93. The Bell 206 particle seperator makes use of individual _____.

94. Each filter is a _____ chamber.

95. Particles move to the outside of the filter by _____ force.

96. Compressor bleed air is used to _____ the particles from the filter.

97. The Bell 212 particle seperator has a seperate _____ for each engine.

98. The particle seperator is _____ open.

99. The particle seperator automatically closes when the:

a. _____

b. _____

100. Air entering the engine has two paths: some air enters the engine while air with particles pass through the _____.

101. Inlet guide vanes are used to _____ the airflow for the compressor.

102. Inlet guide vanes are moveable if the compressor is _____.

103. Damage to the compressor may be the result of:

a. _____

b. _____

104. Nicks and scratches can lead to compressor blade _____.

105. A dirty compressor will result in high operating _____.

106. Blockage of the airflow to the engine can result in stall and _____ of the engine.

107. Acceleration time of turbine engines is _____ than that of reciprocating engines.

108. To assist in acceleration time, most turbo shaft engines use one of the following systems:

a. _____

b. _____

c. _____

109. These devices _____ the compressor during acceleration.

110. All of these systems are usually operated by the _____ and air pressure ratio.

111. Most of the helicopter engines utilize an annular combustor with _____ flow.

112. Most turbine engines _____ the ignition once the engine is running.

113. The fuel control shown in fig. 8-20 of the textbook has a fuel pump driven by the_____.

114. The fuel is routed from the pump to the _____ where some of the fuel will be used to operate a hydraulic system within the control.

115. Fuel leaving the servo filter takes two paths: one to the _____ and the other is to the _____ valve.

116. The relief valve returns fuel to the _____ of the pump.

117. The change over valve directs fuel to either the _____ or _____ mode of the fuel control.

118. The position of the change over valve is controlled by a _____.

119. In the automatic mode, fuel goes from the change over valve to the _____.

120. The pressure regulator valve operates on a _____ of pressure.

121. The fuel flows from the pressure regulator to the _____ valve.

122. The position of the metering valve is determined by a _____.

123. The foot valve is actually a _____ valve.

124. In the manual postion, fuel is routed past a _____ and to a manual metering valve.

125. The mechanical computer section of the fuel control is made up of:

    a. _____

    b. _____

    c. _____

    d. _____

    e. _____

    f. _____

126. Free trubines require both an _____ governor and a _____ governor.

127. Temperature is corrected for by a temperature _____ at the _____ of the engine.

128. The _____ in the temperature compensator moves mechanical linkage that positions the _____ valve.

129. The pressure compensator bellows, operates the metering valve linkage through a _____ _____ valve and _____ operating on fuel pressure.

130. The N_1 governer is a mechanical _____ governor.

131. The N_2 governer is driven from the _____.

132. The three D cam has the fuel schedules _____ into three surfaces of the cam.

133. The airflow and ignition system are in operation prior to _____ to the combustor.

134. Movement of the twist grip operates the:

    a. _____

    b. _____

    c. _____

135. During starting, the _____ continues to operate until the engine is self sustaining.

136. The rotor rpm may be varied by the _____.

137. This adjustment of the rotor rpm is done to meet the particular conditions by use of a _____ _____ which moves the speeder spring of the governor.

138. When the collective is raised, the governor senses an _____ speed condition which demands _____ fuel.

139. Most ignition systems are _____ discharge systems.

140. Many ignition systems have an _____ device in case of flame out.

141. The oldest of the helicopter turboshaft engines is the _____.

142. The five major sections of the T5313 are:

    a. _____

    b. _____

    c. _____

    d. _____

    e. _____

143. The T5313 has variable _____ guide vanes.

144. The compressor of the T53 is made up of five stages of _____ compressor and

one stage of _____ compressor.

145. The _____ converts high velocity air to high pressure air.

146. Bleed air from the diffusor may be used for:

a. _____

b. _____

c. _____

147. Air entering the combustor is used for two purposes which are:

a. _____

b. _____

148. Fuel enters the combustion chamber through 22 atomizers at the _____ end of the

combustor.

149. Gasses flowing out the combustor pass over the _____ compressor turbine

and the _____ power turbine.

150. The power turbine drives a shaft passing through the _____.

151. The power turbine shaft drives the:

a. _____ _____

b. _____

c. _____

152. The gas producer turbine turns the:

a. _____

b. _____

153. The major operating systems of the engine are:

a. _____

b. _____

c. _____

d. _____

e. _____

154. The purpose of the variable inlet guide vanes is to change the _____ of the air entering the compressor.

155. The guide vanes are positioned by a _____ operated by the guide vane actuator.

156. The guide vane actuator is positioned by the _____.

157. For steady state operation the vanes will _____ position.

158. The interstage airbleed improves acceleration by _____ air during acceleration.

159. Bleed holes are provided around the _____ stage of compression.

160. The band is closed through an actuator which operates from pressure of the _____ _____.

161. The control of the interstage air bleed is operated through the _____ as a function of N_1.

162. Anti-icing air is provided to anti-ice the:

a. _____

b. _____

163. The anti-icing air is taken from the _____ through an inline valve.

164. Air exiting the inlet housing struts is _____.

165. The T5313 engine uses a high _____ discharge system.

166. Four _____ are placed in the combustor.

167. The fuel control unit consists of two sections:

a. _____

b. _____

168. The fuel _____ is driven by the N_1 gearbox.

169. Starting fuel is received from the fuel _____.

170. The starting fuel valve routes fuel into a _____ manifold to four starting fuel nozzles which are located at 2, 4, 8, and 10 o'clock positions of the combustor.

171. The main fuel system consists of:

    a. _____

    b. _____

    c. _____

    d. _____

172. The overspeed trip system is designed to prevent an _____ of the N_2 system.

173. When 110% N_2 is reached, the _____ closes a solenoid and limits the fuel.

174. The fuel divider provides both _____ and _____ fuel flow to the atomizers.

175. The fuel manifold is a two section unit with _____ atomizers attached to each section.

176. The oil pump for the T5313 is located on the _____.

177. One element of the pump delivers oil under pressure and the other element delivers _____ _____ oil.

178. Oil for the lubrication system is stored in a _____ mounted tank.

179. The oil filter is a _____ wafer-disc type filter.

180. Oil from the various parts of the engine collect in the _____ and is pumped to the oil cooler before returning to the _____.

181. The most widely used engine on helicopters is the _____ series of engines.

182. The two models of the Allison 250 engine that do no use an axial-centrifugal compressor is the _____ and _____ engine.

183. The major assemblies of the Allison 250 are:

    a. _____

    b. _____

c. _____

d. _____

e. _____

184. The compressor of most models of the Allison 250 have _____ of axial compression and one stage of _____ compressor.

185. The schroll assembly has provisions for _____ and ducts air to the _____ section.

186. The combustor section consists of an outercase, a _____ a single fuel nozzle and _____.

187. The turbine assembly is mounted between the _____ and the_____ _____.

188. The turbine assembly consists of a _____ gas producer turbine and a two stage _____ turbine.

189. A single gearbox is used by the Allison 250 which is powered by the _____ _____ and the _____.

190. The gas producer gear train drives:

a. _____

b. _____

c. _____

d. _____

191. The power turbine gear train powers:

a. _____

b. _____

c. _____

192. The gear type oil pump of the Allison 250 is made up of one pressure element and _____ _____ scavaged elements.

193. Oil leaving the sump area is taken to the _____ before returning the oil to the tank.

194. The oil filter assembly contains:

    a. _____

    b. _____

    c. _____

195. The compressor of the Allison 250 is unloaded by the use of an airbleed _____

    _____.

196. This valve is open during starting and _____ operation.

197. The valve becomes fully closed only when Px becomes equal to _____.

198. The anti-icing system provides hot air from the _____ to the front support area.

199. The anti-icing valve is a _____ valve operated by the pilot.

200. Hot air is exhausted through _____ in the struts and the _____ of the engine.

201. The dual element fuel pump used on the Allison 250 consists of the following:

    a. _____

    b. _____

    c. _____

    d. _____

    e. _____

202. The fuel pump delivers fuel to the gas producer _____.

203. The fuel control lever is positioned by the _____.

204. The basic positions of the twist grip are:

    a. _____

    b. _____

    c. _____

205. The gas producer fuel control automatically meters fuel as a function of compressor _____

    _____ and N_2 rpm.

206. The power turbine governor is not required for _____ or_____

_____ operation.

207. The gas producer and power turbine governor are interconnected by three lines:

a. _____

b. _____

c. _____

208. The power turbine governor is required to control the speed of the _____.

209. The power turbine governor lever is positioned by the _____ and the

_____.

210. The beeper system is used by the pilot to set _____ N_2 rpm.

211. The droop compensator moves the governor anytime the _____ is raised

or lowered.

212. When the power turbine tries to exceed 100%, the turbine governor resets the _____

_____ and limits the fuel flow.

213. When collective pitch is increased, the procedure is reversed and fuel flow is _____

_____ to maintain a constant rpm.

214. The fuel nozzle is a dual orifice type delivering _____ and secondary fuel to the

combustor.

215. The ignition system of the Allison 250 is composed of three units:

a. _____

b. _____

c. _____

216. TOT is the abbreviation for _____.

217. The TOT system operates a self generated electrical impulses from _____

wired in parallel.

218. The PT6-3 engine is a _____ configuration.

219. The PT6-3 engine consists of three major sections: two _____ and one output _____.

220. The compressor section of the PT6-3 consists of a _____ stage axial compressor and a single stage _____ compressor.

221. The PT6-3 combustor is an annular _____ type.

222. An accessory gearbox section mounts to the _____ of each power section.

223. The gearbox drives the following:

    a. _____

    b. _____

    c. _____

224. The lubrication system components for each engine is contained in the _____.

225. Each power turbine shaft is connected to a single gearbox and _____.

226. This gearbox is often referred to as a _____ gearbox.

227. A three stage geartrain is provided for _____ power section.

228. Each power section reduction has its own _____ to prevent one engine from driving the other.

229. Each power section has its own _____ fuel control.

230. Each of these fuel controls are attached to a common _____ control unit.

231. The fuel pump which is used by the engine is a _____ type pump.

232. The manual fuel control unit is controlled by the _____ lever.

233. The automatic fuel control establishes the fuel schedule in response to the _____ _____ requirements.

234. The torque control unit receives _____ from both power sections.

235. The torque control unit controls governor _____. Both engines are limited in torque output and produce _____ torques.

92

236. The flow divider provides fuel to the _____ and _____
_____ fuel manifolds.

237. The PT6-3 has _____ separate oil systems.

238. Each power section has its own lubrication system. The third system is the _____
_____.

239. Cooling air for the lubrication systems is provided by _____ on each power section.

240 Each power section contains an _____ system to
improve the anti-stall characteristics.

241. Some PT6-3 installations provide a dual twist grip for the fuel controls. The upper twist grip
controls _____ engine.

242. The droop compensator maintains rotor rpm as the collective pitch is _____ and
_____.

243. Some helicopters have twin engine installations with _____ shafts to one
transmission.

244. This type of installation requires that the transmission be able to turn with _____
_____ inoperative.

245. Torque is the measurement of _____ of turbine engines.

246. The engine will only produce the power required by the _____ system.

247. Some helicopters are torque limited by the _____ components.

248. Helicopters using a lever arrangement for N_1 speed normally have three operating positions. These
are:

a. _____

b. _____

c. _____

249. On direct shaft turbines, no linkage connects the _____ and fuel control.

250. In autorotation, the lift and rotor rpm is the result of the _____ through the rotor.

251. Many turbine powered helicopters have an _____ warning system. This system usually has a light and horn when N_1 deteriorates.

252. The life of a turbine engine is based on the hours of operation and the _____ of the engine.

253. Many engines are overhauled on a _____ concept.

254. Misalignment between the engine and transmission will shorten the _____ life.

255. Alignment is usually accomplished by _____ the engine mount.

256. Fine adjustment to the engine rigging are normally made after the _____ test.

257. On free turbine installations _____ and _____ systems must be rigged.

258. On the Bell 205, the N_1 system is controlled by the _____. The N_2 system is controlled by the _____ movement..

259. The functions of the twist grip are:

    a. _____

    b. _____

    c. _____

    d. _____

260. The 205 has a flight _____ to prevent engine shutdown in flight.

261. The linier actuator should have a definite length to the stroke. This stroke is moved by the _____ button.

Chapter IX
Tail Rotors

1. The tail rotor is sometimes referred to as the _____ rotor.

2. If the tail rotor system is not used, other methods of anti-torque must be used such as:

   a. _____

   b. _____

   c. _____

3. Tail rotors must use some of the same features which are found in main rotors which include:

   a. _____

   b. _____

4. Tail rotor blades have _____ and _____ pitch.

5. Direction control is obtained by using _____ pedals to change the blade pitch.

6. The power for the tail rotor is furnished through the _____ of the helicopter.

7. When the engine is not operating, the tail rotor is driven by the main _____.

8. The tail rotor shafting must have _____ to move with the tail boom of the helicopter.

9. Shafting for the tail rotor is supported by _____.

10. Alignment of the tail rotor shafting is important because of _____.

11. When tail rotor shafting must be diverted, it is usually done through an intermediate _____ _____.

12. Most often this direction change does not involve an _____ or decrease in speed.

13. The tail rotor gear box may be used to _____ or _____ speed for the tail rotor.

14. The tail rotor always turns _____ than the main rotor.

15. Tail rotor blades may be made of:

   a. _____

   b. _____

16. Some tail rotor pitch change systems utilize _____ as is used on cyclic and collective.

17. The Bell 47 tail rotor drive shaft system is made up of _____ sections.

18. The Bell 47 tail rotor gearbox changes direction 90° and _____ the speed.

19. Couplings between the forward shaft and the mid shaft allow for momentary _____ _____ of the transmission and shafting.

20. The hanger bearings used on the Bell 47 require _____.

21. The aft shaft has a _____ attached to the aft end.

22. The extension tube housing attaches to the _____ and the _____.

23. The Bell 47 tail rotor gearbox output shaft is master splined to index the _____ _____ mechanism.

24. To change the rotory action of the pitch change to a linier motion, an _____ _____ is an integral part of the pitch change shaft.

25. Tail rotor blades used on the Bell 47 are made of _____ construction.

26. Pitch change of the Bell 47 tail rotor bearings are provided by the use of _____ _____ bearings.

27. The delta hinge movement of the Bell 47 is accomplished by the _____ in the _____ assembly.

28. The pitch change horns on the Bell 47 also have provisions for _____ _____ to control pedal creep.

29. The Hughes 500 uses a _____ tail rotor drive shaft.

30. Halfway down the Hughes 500 drive shaft is located a _____ dampener.

31. The dampener consists of a _____ centered _____ block.

32. The Hughes 500 shaft is balanced with _____ weights _____ to the

shafts.

33. Unlike the Bell 47, the Hughes 500 gear box is a speed _____ rather than

speed _____.

34. The two blade assemblies are connected to a _____.

35. On the output shaft of the Hughes 500 tail rotor gear box is a _____ which

is controlled by the foot pedals.

36. The Hughes 500 tail rotor blades have a _____ spar.

37. The Hughes 500 tail rotor hub consists of:

a. _____

b. _____

c. _____

d. _____

38. The drive fork is used to transfer torque from the gearbox to the _____.

39. _____ are used to center the drive fork in the hub.

40. The pitch links are forged aluminum with replaceable swaged _____ bearings.

41. The "A" Star 350 has a _____ piece tail rotor drive shaft.

42. The drive shafts of the "A" Star 350 are connected to each other and tail rotor gearbox by _____

_____ couplings.

43. The forward couplings are larger because more _____ occurs at the transmission

and engine.

44. The hanger bearings on the "A" Star 350 operate on rubber sleeves in order to _____

vibration.

45. The tail rotor gearbox used on the "A" Star has a speed _____ as well as a directional change.

46. The "A" Star makes use of a _____ seal for oil control.

47. The pitch change mechanism is mounted to the _____ and is free to slide with the pedal input.

48. The tail rotor on the "A" Star is made of _____.

49. The tail rotor has no conventional _____ or _____ bearings.

50. The two blades are molded to a _____ spar.

51. The blades have an _____ bearing between the half-shells.

52. The bearings are capable of carrying both _____ and sheer loads.

53. The blade spar is allowed to _____ freely because the cavity surrounding the spar is filled with a _____.

54. The Bell 212 has _____ driveshafts for the tail rotor system.

55. All of the driveshafts are the same length except _____.

56. Each shaft has a _____ coupling riveted to each end.

57. Each shaft has weights bonded to the shaft for _____.

58. The V band type clamps securing the curvic coupling are installed _____ _____ to the bolts of the preceding clamp.

59. Each of the hangers is built to allow flexing on the _____ of the hanger.

60. The flexible couplings are lubricated by _____.

61. The alignment of the driveshaft is insured by _____ bonded to the tail boom.

62. The 42° gearbox may have either drive quill replaced without disturbing the _____ and _____.

63. The 90° gearbox is a speed. _____.

64. The case of the 90° gearbox utilizes ground _____ for the placement of the quills.

65. The hub of the tail rotor is _____ and _____ as is the main rotor.

66. The yoke of the 212 tail rotor is a _____ .

67. The tail rotor blades bolt to the yoke on _____ type bearings which provide the _____ axis of the blade.

68. The 212 rotor blades are balanced against a _____ at manufacture.

69. The pitch change of the 212 tail rotor is assisted by _____ .

70. The impending failure of a bearing will always be indicated by a rise in _____ of the bearing package.

71. Bearing failures of the tail rotor system are always accompanied with _____ _____ vibration.

72. In order to warn the pilot of high bearing temperature, the exposed shafts are often _____ _____ on post flight to determine a temperature rise.

73. Enclosed shafts often use heat sensitive _____ as a warning device.

74. The Bell 206 uses a bearing hanger that allows the bearing to _____ in the hanger if the bearing should freeze.

75. Particular attention to the ends of the drive shafts should be taken during inspection to check the _____ , _____ and bonding.

76. Couplings made of stainless steel discs require special attention to the _____ _____ during disassembly and assembly.

77. Misalignment of the tail rotor shafting will cause _____ levels to increase.

78. Most newer helicopters have _____ permanently bonded to the tail boom in order to align the tail boom.

79. Runout checks of the tail rotor shafting is done with the shafting _____ on the helicopter.

80. The hangers are _____ in order to correct for misalignment.

99

81. The lubricant used in the newer helicopter's gearboxes is usually the same as the _____.

82. Tail rotors on newer helicopters often require no lubrication due to the use of _____ _____ and sealed bearings.

83. Many parts of the tail rotor are assigned a _____ due to the stresses placed on them.

84. Tail rotor vibrations are always _____ frequency.

85. The vibration problem can often be isolated to the _____ or _____ _____ system by moving the pedals.

86. The drive shafts are usually _____ balanced at manufacture.

87. The tail rotor will require _____ balance and _____ balance in the field.

88. The placement of weight in other than authorized locations on the tail rotor would be _____.

89. Many of the older tail rotor blades add spanwise weight to the blade _____ and cordwise weight to the _____ trailing edge surface.

90. Most newer tail rotors add weight to the _____ area rather than the blades.

91. The universal balancer utilizes a disc and cable attached to the arbor which is dampened with _____ _____.

92. When the tail rotor is balanced, a circle will be formed between the _____ _____ and _____ when using the universal balancer.

93. All static balancing must be acomplished in a _____ in order to insure accuracy.

94. The Bell 206 balancer utilizes a _____ placed on a mandral to give movement in all directions.

95. Some of the older helicopters use _____ or a _____ _____ stand similar to those used for propellers.

96. Blades using this type of stand are placed in the _____ position to check spanwise balance.

97. The greater accuracy in the static balance, the less _____ balance problems will occur.

98. Track of the tail rotor blades is established before any _____ balance is attempted.

99. Some helicopters have no provisions for tail rotor _____ adjustment.

100. The helicopter must be operating at _____ speed when tracking by the stick method.

101. The stick should enter the tail rotor near the _____ of the blade.

102. If only one blade is marked, the _____ link must be adjusted.

103. The links may be adjusted _____ or _____ with no adverse effect on the operation.

104. If a large correction is necessary, _____ blades should be adjusted rather than one.

105. Reflective tape is placed on the blade _____ when using the electronic method of tracking.

106. When the tail rotor is viewed from the side, the "strobex" is adjusted until _____ images are visible on a two bladed rotor.

107. If the rotor is in track, the images of the reflective tape will be _____ forming a +.

108. The adjustments for track are the _____ regardless of the method for checking the track.

109. Dynamic balance of the tail rotor is done with the _____ and _____ units.

110. The phazor portion of the _____ unit is not used.

111. The tail rotor blade marked with the reflective tape is known as the _____ blade.

112. The vibrex unit must be tuned to the _____ rpm before the vibration level is measured.

113. In checking the tail rotor vibration, the target blade is viewed with the strobex to determine the _____ of the vibration.

114. The _____ chart is read in the same manner as the main rotor chart.

115. All track and balance checks must be accomplished in _____ weather conditions.

116. Most helicopters use a _____ tube system for tail rotor pitch control.

117. To add feel to the tail rotor when hydraulic boost is used, some helicopters use _____ _____.

118. The Bell 212 has a hydraulic boost, _____ and a _____ _____ on the pitch change tail rotor.

119. Many of the newer helicopters are rigged to the _____ positions rather than the neutral.

120. On some helicopters, _____ creep is adjustable.

121. If the left pedal moves forward when the foot pressure is released, the weights are _____ _____.

Chapter X
Airframes And Related Systems

1. Some of the early helicopters used _____ steel fuselages.

2. In addition to the cost of manufacture, it was difficult to hold close _____ with this type of fuselage.

3. Aluminum structures were of the _____ and _____ design as used in many fixed wing aircraft.

4. Some helicopters were manufactured with a combination of _____ structure and _____ structure.

5. Bonded structures include a variety of materials including:

   a. _____

   b. _____

   c. _____

6. Bonding eliminates the need for _____ and _____ which is required on older forms of construction.

7. Todays helicopters are usually a _____ of materials using each to its best advantage.

8. The structure of helicopters varies from fixed wing aircraft because of the _____ and _____ locations.

9. The helicopter has both the _____ and _____ acting on the same point.

10. Many helicopters use a _____ landing gear.

11. The _____ levels of the helicopter are great because of the rotating components.

12. The _____ and _____ have reduced airframe vibration levels.

13. The tail boom of the helicopter is stressed with side loads by the _____.

14. Additional downward loads are placed on the tail boom by the _____ _____.

15. The wheel and skid gear have advantages and disadvantages which are:

    a. _____

    b. _____

    c. _____

    d. _____

16. The pilot requires great vislbility in the front of the helicopter because of _____ angles.

17. The body structure of the "A" Star is the _____ member of the fuselage.

18. The body member carries both the _____, _____ and _____.

19. The body member will also support the other _____ members either directly or indirectly.

20. The body member is a reinforced box with _____ placed in each side.

21. The bottom structure is made up of two beams which carry the weight of the _____ and transmit it to the _____ structure.

22. The cabin section is made almost exclusively of _____ materials.

23. The windshields and windows of the "A" Star are made of _____.

24. The rear section of the "A" Star fuselage supports the _____ on the top and the _____ on the rear.

25. The tail boom is of convential design using _____ and stringers to give the needed rigidity.

26. The tail boom is attached by _____.

27. The tail boom has the following items attached:

    a. _____

    b. _____

    c. _____

    d. _____

28. The upper vertical fin is a _____ airfoil while the lower fin is a

    _____ airfoil.

29. The horizontal stabilizer produces a _____ force on the stabilizer.

30. The "A" Star landing gear has a long steel strip attached to the skids and bent downward. This eliminates the possibility of _____.

31. The "A" Star has a fuselage antivibration device. This creates a _____ for

    _____ vibration.

32. The Bell 206 fuselage has _____ main sections.

33. The forward section of the fuselage is constructed of one inch thick honeycomb bonded to an _____

    _____ sheet.

34. The honeycomb structure provides:

    a. _____

    b. _____

    c. _____

35. The bottom of the 206 forward fuselage is often referred to as the _____ assembly.

36. The forward section of the 206 fuselage is the primary area carrying the _____

    and _____ forces.

37. The intermediate section of the fuselage is _____ construction.

38. The intermediate section forms the _____ compartment and supports the _____ on the top portion.

39. The tail boom of the 206 is _____ construction.

40. The tail boom is attached to the intermediate section by _____.

41. The vertical fin of the 206 is used to _____ the tail rotor in forward flight.

42. The horizontal stabilizer is an _____ airfoil.

43. The Hughes 500 fuselage uses _____ materials.

44. The strength of the Hughes 500 fuselage is obtained by a _____ construction.

45. The main strength member of the Hughes 500 fuselage is the _____.

46. The four major bulkheads of the Hughes 500 fuselage support the following:

    a. The first bulkhead _____

    b. The second _____

    c. The third bulkhead _____

    d. The fourth bulkhead _____

47. The front and aft canted frames are tied together by the _____.

48. This tie forms a _____ which is the major strength component of the fuselage.

49. The crashworthiness of the Hughes 500 fuselage include such features as:

    a. _____

    b. _____

    c. _____

    d. _____

50. Structural repair information may be found either in the _____ manual or in a _____ manual.

51. _____ are often necessary for major repairs because of alignment.

52. Misalignment of the fuselage will cause:

    a. Shortened life of the _____

    b. Shortened life of the _____

53. Hard landings often require _____ of the structure.

54. Such areas of the structure would include:

   a. _____

   b. _____

   c. _____

   d. _____

55. Hard landings may also result in damage to _____ components.

56. Sudden stoppage of the main rotor is defined as _____

   _____.

57. Sudden stoppage forces can be transmitted throughout the _____ and

   _____ components.

58. Sudden stoppage of the rotor head could include:

   a. _____

   b. _____

   c. _____

59. Sudden stoppage of the tail rotor could lead to secondary damage including:

   a. _____

   b. _____

   c. _____

60. Some helicopters require the rejection of the _____ if the tail rotor

   blades are damaged.

61. Airframe systems which would be similar to those used on fixed wing aircraft would include:

   a. _____

   b. _____

   c. _____

62. Most helicopter fuel systems are _____ type systems.

63. The Bell 206 system incorporates a single _____ tank.

64. The Bell 206 has two boost pumps which supply fuel through a _____ fuel line.

65. The 206 shutoff is _____ operated.

66. Many turbine powered helicopters utilize a system in which _____ nicad batteries are used during starting.

67. ECU stands for _____.

68. Special equipment for helicopters are produced by the manufacturer or individuals holding _____ _____.

69. One of the advantages of high skid gear is _____ when landing in unapproved areas.

70. Most helicopters which make over water flights will be equipped with _____ for emergencies.

71. Cargo hooks are used when _____ loads are carried by the helicopter.

72. The cargo hoist has both a _____ and _____ release.

73. External loads may often _____ the normal gross weight in a restricted category.

74. The Bell 206 requires that the door post _____ for litter installation.

75. Spraying equipment is _____ built by the aircraft manufacturer.

Answers to Chapter I

1. three
2. Bell 47
3. 1974
4. Franklin, Lycoming
5. two, four
6. 47G4A
7. 204B
8. UH-1
9. T539A, T5311A
10. 204
11. 15
12. 9500
13. T5313A
14. Jet Ranger
15. Allison
16. 5,7
17. twin
18. 412
19. PT6-3
20. 11,200 lbs.
21. 222
22. LTS101
23. 615
24. 10
25. UH-12
26. reciprocating, turbine
27. Franklin

28. 12L
29. 4
30. FH1100
31. Allison
32. 5
33. 269
34. Lycoming
35. three
36. horizontally
37. 0360
38. Hughes 500
39. Allison 250
40. 4, 5
41. 152
42. 5
43. S51
44. S55
45. Pratt and Whitney
46. 7200
47. H34
48. Wright Cyclone
49. 14
50. PT6 Twinback
51. special purpose
52. 42,000
53. corporate
54. Allison

55. four
56. General Electric
57. 19,500
58. 5
59. 2
60. Lycoming
61. 305
62. 1965
63. three
64. 280
65. 0360
66. tandem
67. B0105
68. rigid
69. Aerospatiale
70. turbine
71. Alouette
72. Turbomeca
73. 4
74. Astuzou
75. 170
76. twin
77. 14
78. Puma
79. 20
80. Lycoming

Answers to Chapter II

1. a. forward
   b. backward
   c. sideways
   d. hover
   e. vertically
2. maintenance, trouble-shooting
3. main rotor
4. lift, thrust
5. root, tip
6. leading, trailing
7. flight characteristics
8. symmetrical
9. symmetrical
10. relative wind
11. backward
12. advancing
13. retreating
14. a. movement of the rotor blades
    b. horizontal movement of the helicopter
    c. flapping of the rotor blade
    d. wind speed and direction
15. chord, reference
16. collective
17. angle of attack
18. chord line, relative wind
19. relative wind, pitch
20. relative wind, gravity
21. drag
22. angle of attack
23. velocity
24. center of pressure
25. center of pressure

26. instability
27. center of pressure
28. stall, airfoil, reverse flow
29. lift, stall
30. power
31. density
32. a. temperature
    b. altitude
    c. humidity
33. altitude
34. hot day, cold day
35. pitch, power
36. thrust
37. thrust, drag
38. droop
39. centrifugal
40. lift, centrifugal
41. coning
42. rotor disc, path plane
43. thrust
44. thrust
45. forward
46. angle of attack
47. feathering
48. collective
49. equal
50. cyclic
51. tilt
52. mass
53. gyroscopic precession
54. 90 degrees
55. swashplate
56. Newton's third
57. rotation

58. a. tail rotor system
    b. co-axial rotors
    c. tandem rotors
    d. side by side rotors
    e. hot blade system
59. tail rotor
60. tail rotor
61. foot pedals, pitch
62. power
63. vertical fin
64. is not
65. tip, root
66. twist
67. angle of attack, faster
68. advancing, retreating
69. lift
70. dissymetry
71. flapping hinge
72. seesaw
73. upward
74. speed up
75. geometric
76. lead-lag
77. chordwise
78. forward
79. center of gravity
80. aft
81. dampeners
82. underslung
83. mast, flexibility, geometric
84. a. rigid
    b. semi rigid
    c. fully articulated

85. semi rigid, fully articulated

86. rigid

87. flapping, lead lag

88. feathering, flap

89. corriolis effect

90. feathering, flapping hinge, lead lag

91. a. simplified construction
    b. subject to wind gusts
    c. semi rigid requires underslinging
    a. complex construction
    b. smoother operation
    c. high centrifugal hinge loads

92. tail rotor thrust

93. a. tilt in the mast assembly
    b. rigging of the cyclic

94. one half

95. dense, air cushion

96. forward speed

97. additional

98. increased efficiency

99. 15 - 20

100. increased drag on the fuselage

101. flight

102. downwash

103. rear

104. 2:1 vibration, lateral cyclic

105. fore, aft

106. flapping hinges

107. stall characteristics

108. a. insufficient airspeed
     b. too great of an angle of attack
     c. heavy wing load

109. faster

110. angle of attack

111. heavy

112. temperature, altitude, maneuvers

113. retreating

114. vibration

115. pitch up

116. a. reduce forward speed
     b. reduce pitch of the rotor
     c. increase rotor speed

117. lift, airflow

118. downward

119. upward

120. 25 - 75%

121. propeller, drag force

122. rpm

123. flare, aft

124. altitude, forward speed

125. unsafe

126. a. density altitude
     b. maximum weight

127. self-excited

128. destroy

129. fully articulated

130. lead lag

131. center of gravity

132. a. one wheel landings
     b. slope landings
     c. a flat strut or tire

133. take off

134. disturbed

135. move in the direction

136. behavior

137. stable, unstable

138. a. the rotor disc will follow the fuselage
     b. a change in speed will cause the rotor to tilt
     c. a change in rotor speed will cause the center of gravity to oscillate and tilt the fuselage

139. stabilizer bar

140. independent

141. dynamic instability

142. a. cyclic
     b. collective
     c. anti-torque pedals

143. altitude

144. increase

145. correlation

146. compensating cam

147. pitch

148. take off

149. left

150. directional

151. a. off set vertical fin
     b. the ducted fan tail rotor

152. tip path plane

153. pitch

154. gyroscopic precession

155. horizontal stabilizer

Answers to Chapter III

1. fixed wing
2. additional
3. 27, 29
4. transport
5. additional
6. 43
7. finate
8. The helicopter must be maintained in accordance to manufacturer's instructions
9. the aircraft is maintained in accordance to the FAR
10. equipment list
11. a. kits
    b. service bulletins
    c. supplemental type certificates
12. retirement
13. historical
14. finate
15. owner operator
16. maintenance technician
17. replaced
18. a. sheet method
    b. card method
    c. computor method
19. helicopters, components
20. a. part number
    b. serial number
    c. aircraft time when installed
    d. component time when installed
    e. hour life of the component
    f. time when the component is to be removed
21. component
22. AD

23. overhaul
24. one
25. maintenance
26. 6331.5
27. 3828.5
28. 4339.2
29. was not
30. unlimited
31. 600
32. 300
33. separate listing
34. carbon
35. so that maintenance trends may be analyzed and schedules for maintenance may be planned.
36. manufacturer
37. companies
38. ATA
39. company
40. flight
41. limitations
42. first
43. second
44. third
45. second
46. fourth
47. fifth
48. ATA System, manufacturer's format
49. ATA
50. maintenance, overhaul
51. field
52. equipment
53. exhange
54. microfiche
55. subscription

56. first
57. component
58. a. general description
    b. trouble shooting
    c. removal
    d. teardown inspection
    e. reassembly
    f. installation
59. system
60. model, manufacturer
61. chapter
62. components
63. a. chapter
    b. section
    c. subject
64. two
65. a. use of the manual
    b. parts ordering information
    c. vendor codes
    d. index of sections
66. first
67. four
68. sub assemblies
69. figure
70. fourth
71. usage
72. cross reference index
73. maintenance
74. maintenance
75. field problems
76. airworthiness directives
77. manufacturer
78. service letters
79. operator
80. modifications
81. FAA
82. anyone

Answers to Chapter IV

1. tail
2. right
3. color
4. red, white
5. skid
6. a. bar must be used to raise and lower the wheels
   b. the bar must be secure in the wheel unit
   c. personnel must be clear of the bar
   d. hands and feet must be clear of the skid gear
   e. locking devices must be in place before the bar is released
   f. helicopters cannot be started with the wheels down
7. upward, downward
8. platform
9. a. sufficient help must be available to view all parts of the helicopter
   b. towing must be accomplished smoothly with no jerky motion
   c. all rotating components must be secure
   d. tow bar turning radii must be observed
10. prevailing
11. retracted
12. jackpoints
13. rotor
14. flexing
15. inlet, exhaust
16. mast
17. lifting points
18. jackpoints
19. extensions

20. value
21. thrust
22. a. width
    b. outer diameter
    c. bore
    d. shoulder
    e. inner race
    f. seperator
    g. outer race
23. lubrication
24. may not
25. ball
26. radial
27. tapered
28. light
29. control
30. a. dry film
    b. grease
31. threaded
32. trammel
33. aligned
34. roller staking
35. swagged
36. lubrication
37. grease
38. high, low
39. operating
40. splash, spray
41. transmission
42. sight guage
43. lubrication, method, frequency
44. clean
45. arbor press
46. maintenance
47. inner

48. heat
49. duplex
50. V
51. thrust side
52. back to back, face to face tandem
53. a. tandem
    b. back to back
    c. face to face
54. tandem
55. face to face, back to back
56. face to face
57. oil bath
58. interference, pinch
59. .026
60. elastomeric
61. rotational
62. rotor heads
63. lubricant
64. synthetic
65. elastomer, metal
66. a. spherical
    b. conical
    c. radial
    d. axial
    e. cylindrical
67. a. no lubrication
    b. no disassembly
    c. no seizure
    d. long service life
    e. no brinnelling or pitting
    f. reduction of vibration
    g. boot and seals are eliminated
    h. controlled stiffness
68. cost, size
69. flap, change, rigid

70. a. transmit power
    b. change direction
    c. change speed
71. a. straight tooth gear
    b. helical gear
    c. spiral gear
72. lash, pattern
73. break

74. lubricated
75. C
76. A is the toe
    B is the heel
77. print
78. heel, toe
79. load

80. helical
81. B
82. altered
83. shims
84. lash
85. replaced

Answers to Chapter V

1. a. centrifugal
   b. vibration
   c. twisting
   d. flexing
2. advantages, disadvantages
3. semi rigid, fully articulating
4. least
5. semi rigid
6. semi rigid
7. flapping axis
8. pitch change
9. fully articulated
10. dampener
11. grease
12. fiberglass
13. yoke
14. drag braces
15. adapter nut
16. trunnion
17. tension torsion plates
18. incidence arms
19. oil
20. precone
21. fine wire

22. spanwise
23. latch
24. lead lag, flapping
25. ball bearings
26. droop stop
27. hydraulic
28. stationary
29. tapered roller
30. shoe
31. a. centrifugal loads
    b. flapping action
    c. feathering action
32. vibration
33. five, four
34. mechanical, elastomeric
35. elastomeric
36. bifilar
37. spindle
38. elastomeric
39. fiberglass
40. finite
41. flexing
42. distorsion
43. vibration
44. rigid

45. flex
46. a. wood
    b. metal
    c. composite
47. wooden
48. laminated
49. mass balance
50. fiberglass
51. abrasion
52. cheekplates
53. gravity, pressure
54. tip pocket
55. pairs
56. balance
57. finite
58. operating
59. rebalance
60. exchanged
61. metal
62. single blades
63. finite
64. a. even distribution of stresses
    b. smoother contours
    c. flexible joints
    d. reduced weight

65. aluminum

66. span

67. inertia

68. honeycomb

69. doublers

70. BIS

71. BIM

72. color

73. bonding

74. stresses

75. root, outboard

76. honeycomb

77. rental

78. fiberglass

79. metal

80. life

81. notch

82. lubrication

83. stressed

84. historical records

85. overspeeds, stopage, landings

86. blades, blade

87. pitch change

88. multiplier

89. supported

90. pins

91. blade racks

92. 10ths

93. magnaflux

94. embrittlement

95. discretion

96. identification

97. gravity

98. semi rigid

99. forward

100. alignment

101. angle

102. mirrors

103. relationship

104. scope

105. static

106. chordwise, spanwise

107. chordwise

108. drafts

109. filled

110. a. to the blade tip pocket
    b. inside the blade bolt

111. disturbed

112. aft

113. main rotors, tail rotors

114. vibration

115. imbalance

116. dynamic

117. displacement, amplitude

118. frequency

119. frequency, amplitude

120. sympathetic

121. natural

122. transit

123. a. low frequency
    b. medium frequency
    c. high frequency

124. low

125. 1:1

126. lateral, vertical

127. vertical

128. lateral

129. identifiable

130. medium

131. medium

132. high

133. stationary

134. wear factors

135. tip path plane

136. a. stick method
    b. flag method
    c. light reflector
    d. pre-track method
    e. electronic

137. ground

138. in-flight

139. windy

140. Figure A shows the blades in track
    Figure B requires that the red blade be lowered or the white blade must be raised
    Figure C requires the same adjustment as Figure B

141. ground

142. blade tips

143. Figure A is in track
    Figure B requires the blue blade to be raised or the red blade to be lowered
    Figure C requires that the blue blade be lowered or red blade raised

144. ground, air

145. Figure A blades are in track

146. pre-track method

147. blade

148. light reflector

149. Figure B shows one blade too high—lower the high blade.
    Figure A shows all blades are in track—No corrective action is needed.
    Figure C shows two blades which are out of track. One is too high and one is too low—lower the high blade and raise the low blade.

150. pitch change

151. angle of attack

152. trim tabs

153. The tab must be bent upward. (Lower figure)

154. neutral

155. airflow

156. climbing blade

157. flight

158. elastic

159. low speed

160. low, high

161. track

162. trial and error

163. taping

164. tape, blade

165. balancing

166. chordwise

167. chordwise, spanwise

168. vibration

169. chordwise

170. chordwise

171. heavy, nugging

172. aft

173. blade

174. aft

175. electronic balancer

176. accelerometer

177. filter

178. inches per second

179. .1

180. magnetic pickup

181. phazor

182. different

183. spanwise, chordwise

184. 5 grams should be added to the blank blade or subtracted from the target blade. The blank blade must be swept aft.

185. spanwise

186. clock corrector

187. lead lag

188. a. hydraulic
 b. multiple disc
 c. elastomeric

189. imbalance

190. hydraulic

191. multiple disc

192. elastomeric

193. 1:1

194. moving the blade by hand about the lead-lag axis

195. strobe light

196. counterweights

197. heavy

198. neutral

199. autorotation

200. retreating blade stall

201. lift developed

202. a. gross weight of the helicopter
 b. density altitude

203. adjusting the length of the pitch change rods equally

Answers to Chapter VI

1. torsional, tension

2. finite

3. stabilizer bar

4. a. main rotor
 b. stabilizer bar
 c. dampener bracket
 d. swash plate
 e. transmission

5. stationary

6. drive shaft

7. tension, compression

8. transmission

9. roller

10. control tubes

11. reworked

12. semi rigid

13. a. dimensionally
 b. magnafluxed
 c. for run out

14. stabilizer bar

15. rigidity

16. rotation

17. dampeners

18. tie rod

19. static

20. 47

21. stabilizer bar

22. delayed

23. quick

24. cyclic, collective

25. pitch

26. swashplate

27. a. left
 b. right
 c. fore
 d. aft

28. swashplate

29. same, 90 degrees

30. precession

31. swashplate

32. mast

33. clean

34. scale

35. boost

36. left

37. collective

38. twist grip

39. compressor

40. a. starter
    b. engine trim
    c. landing lights

41. friction

42. upward

43. all

44. a. radio microphone
    b. aircraft trim

45. base

46. push-pull

47. forked, spherical bearing

48. adjustable

49. sealed

50. steel

51. trammel

52. close tolerance

53. fiber-lock

54. rotary, liniar

55. a. change travel
    b. change mechanical
       advantage

56. mixer box

57. collective, cyclic

58. spring

59. compressed

60. a. cyclic

    b. collective
    c. tail rotors

61. integral

62. magnetic brakes

63. magnetic brake

64. gradient

65. trim

66. spring

67. a. bungee springs
    b. counterweights
    c. control paddles

68. aiding

69. control

70. transmission

71. gauge

72. 2000

73. buttons

74. throwaway

75. piston

76. cylinder

77. irreversible

78. two

79. servo

80. out

81. trapped

82. control

83. boost

84. pump

85. solenoid

86. resevoir

87. energized

88. cyclic

89. dual

90. a. collective
    b. cyclic
    c. tail rotor

91. tail rotor

92. top, bottom

93. do not

94. piston-type

95. 1000

96. pressure, return

97. return

98. solenoid

99. servo, by-pass

100. piston

101. cylinder

102. springs

103. lower actuator

104. upper actuator

105. accumulator

106. irreversible

107. leakage

108. pressure

109. external

110. removal, replacement

111. vibration

112. adjustments

113. pins, jigs

114. neutral

115. position

116. stops

117. collective, cyclic

118. bolt

119. hydraulic

120. rigging

121. fixture

122. gradients

123. cyclic

124. CG Range

Answers to Chapter VII

1. three, four
2. 3000
3. 6600
4. tip, blade
5. high
6. reduce
7. engine
8. vertically
9. nose
10. horizontally
11. adapter
12. single
13. transmission
14. short shaft
15. misalignment
16. grease
17. flexible couplings
18. crown tooth gears
19. springs
20. electrobeam
21. lubrication
22. housing
23. tension
24. stainless steel discs
25. magnetic particle inspection
26. finite
27. a. deterioration
    b. **separation**
    c. deformation
28. failure
29. engine, transmission
30. reciprocating, free
31. starting
32. engine, transmission

33. manually, automatically
34. over running clutch
35. wheeling unit
36. engine
37. transmission, rotor
38. autorotation
39. automatic
40. centrifugal
41. engine
42. transmission
43. mecury
44. air
45. slippage
46. oil
47. dry
48. free wheeling
49. 29000
50. belt tightener
51. pilot
52. solenoid
53. overspeed
54. hydro-mechanical
55. fluid
56. engine oil
57. driven
58. free wheeling
59. transmission
60. drive system
61. autorotation
62. sprag
63. one
64. a. an inner race
    b. an outer race
    c. sprags

65. 8
66. greater
67. engaged
68. outer, inner
69. sprags
70. pulley
71. output
72. a. transmission accessories
    b. tail rotor
73. transmission
74. front
75. bolts
76. grease
77. oil
78. Gazelle
79. lobed
80. lobe, driver
81. heel
82. turbine
83. turbine
84. engine, transmission
85. power output
86. transmissions
87. optical-electronic
88. deflection
89. drive shaft
90. twist
91. sensor
92. discs
93. disc
94. per cent
95. rotor brake
96. shutdown

97. inertia

98. wear factors

99. transmission

100. hydraulically, manually

101. hydraulic

102. cabin roof

103. dual

104. does not

105. manually

106. fixed, moveable

107. spring, engaged

108. fork

109. tachometer

110. tachometer

111. engine, rotor

112. autorotation

113. tachometer

114. split

115. shoe

116. mercury

117. oil supply

118. wear

119. vibration

120. increased, aggrevated

121. harmonic, sympathetic

122. torsional

123. engine

124. a. an adapter plate
    b. a basket mount
    c. rubber lord mounts
    d. bottom engine mount

125. adapter plate

126. engine, transmission

127. lord mounts

128. sprag mount

129. fore-aft, side

130. safety cable

131. finite

132. deterioration

133. mast

134. flight, vibrations

135. engine

136. pylon mount links

137. isolation mount

138. elastomers

139. original

140. safety

141. alignment

142. two-per revolution

143. fuselage

144. flexture

145. tuning

146. fore, aft

147. lift

148. no

149. spiral bevel, helical

150. planetary

151. a. cooling fan
    b. tail rotor
    c. hydraulic pump
    d. rotor tachometer
    e. generator

152. engine

153. top case

154. lower

155. a. centrifugal clutch
    b. free wheeling unit
    c. two stage planetary system
    d. accessory drive gears

156. oil

157. spider

158. drum

159. sun gear

160. a. lower case bearing
    b. fan quill sleeve
    c. hydraulic pump quill
    d. tail rotor quill
    e. generator quill

161. pedestal

162. three

163. pinion gear

164. two

165. sun gear, accessory

166. planetary

167. free wheeling

168. fixed gear

169. free gear

170. autorotation, locking

171. rollers, spring

172. clockwise

173. pinion

174. mast

175. separate

176. oil

177. pattern, lash

178. 600 hour

179. gauge pins

180. free wheeling

181. main case

182. a. input quill
    b. accessory drive quill
    c. oil pump
    d. the spiral bevel gear

183. transmission

184. triplex

185. spiral bevel

186. gear shaft

187. fixed ring

188. mast

189. one

190. spiral bevel

191. a. transmission oil pump
    b. hydraulic pump
    c. rotor tachometer

192. free wheeling

193. vane

194. lower case

195. a. temperature bulb
    b. an oil bypass valve

196. tail rotor drive

197. bypasses

198. upper, lower

199. sight gauge

200. lash

201. stationary

202. cabin

203. free wheeling, clutch

204. pinion gear

205. engine

206. tail rotor

207. output pinion

208. output pinion

209. spiral bevel

210. right, left

211. spur

212. a. oil pump
    b. filter assembly
    c. rotor tachometer

213. a. external oil cooler
    b. pressure pump
    c. scavenge pump
    d. internal oil filter
    e. by pass valve
    f. oil temperature swith
    g. miscellaneous lines

214. gerotor

215. oil cooler

216. oil temperature

217. main drive shaft

218. throw away

219. input gear shaft

Answers to Chapter VIII

1. fixed wing

2. vertically

3. lubrication

4. higher

5. horsepower

6. fan

7. constant

8. rotor

9. high

10. flywheel

11. vibration

12. Franklin, Lycoming

13. dry sump

14. cooling fan

15. magnetos

16. timing

17. hand crank

18. radial

19. nose

20. inward, upward

21. horizontal

22. ram air

23. front

24. V belts

25. higher

26. fan quill

27. smaller

28. fan

29. shaft, gearbox

30. sheet metal, fiberglass

31. root

32. transient

33. statically

34. buzz

35. collective

36. opposite

37. thumb

38. correlation

39. collective

40. cambox

41. throttle-to-power

42. throttle setting

43. slot

44. engine

45. affect

46. correlation rigging

47. helicopter

48. 300, 300θ

49. turboshaft

50. shaft horsepower

51. gear reduction

52. direct shaft, free shaft

53. free shaft

54. compressor

55. compressor

56. power turbine

57. axial, centrifugal

58. axial

59. reduced

60. increased

61. stator, rotor

62. increases, pressure

63. larger

64. combustion

65. annular

66. reverse

67. rapidly expands

68. nozzle

69. compressor

70. shaft

71. cold, hot

72. horsepower

73. shaft horsepower

74. benefit

75. excess

76. power

77. demanded

78. pitch

79. manifold

80. torquemeter

81. footpounds

82. rpm, torque

83. compressor, power turbine

84. per cent

85. output shaft rpm, rotor

86. N_1, N_2

87. lower

88. drops

89. exhaust gasses

90. starting

91. not

92. particle separator

93. elements

94. swirl

95. centrifugal

96. scavenge

97. inlet

98. usually

99. a. N_1 rpm drops below 52%
    b. fire extinguisher handle is pulled

100. ejector

101. straighten

102. transsonic

103. a. foreign object damage
    b. erosion

104. failure

105. temperatures

106. flame out

107. slower

108. a. bleed valves
    b. bleed ports
    c. variable stators

109. unload

110. fuel control

111. reverse

112. deactivate

113. gas producer

114. filter

115. relief valve, change over

116. inlet side

117. manual, automatic

118. solenoid

119. pressure regulator

120. differential

121. metering

122. mechanical computer

123. minimum pressure

124. restrictor

125. a. temperature compensator
    b. barometric pressure compensator
    c. N_1 governor
    d. N_2 governor
    e. power control actuator
    f. 3 D cam

126. N_1, N_2

127. bulb, inlet

128. bellows, metering

129. servo, piston

130. flyweight

131. N_2 system

132. ground

133. fuel flow

134. a. N_1 governor
    b. power control actuator
    c. fuel control stopcock

135. starter

136. N_2 governor

137. linear actuator

138. under, more

139. high capacitance

140. automatic relight

141. Lycoming T 53

142. a. air inlet
    b. compressor
    c. diffuser
    d. combustion
    e. exhaust

143. inlet

144. axial, centrifugal

145. diffusor

146. a. cabin heat
    b. oil cooler blower
    c. engine anti-ice

147. a. support combustion
    b. cool the combustor

148. aft

149. two stage, two stage

150. compressor

151. a. gear reduction
    b. engine output shaft
    c. N_2 gearbox

152. a. compressor
    b. accessory gearbox

153. a. variable inlet guide vanes
    b. interstage airbleed
    c. anti-icing system
    d. ignition system
    e. fuel system

154. angle of attack

155. synchronizing ring

156. fuel control

157. assume a steady

158. releasing

159. fifth

160. diffusor

161. fuel control

162. a. inlet housing
    b. inlet guide vanes

163. diffusor

164. dumped overboard

165. capicator

166. ignitors

167. a. the fuel regulator
    b. the overspeed governor

168. regulator

169. regulator

170. two piece

171. a. overspeed trip system
    b. flow divider
    c. main fuel manifold
    d. main fuel atomizers

172. overspeed

173. speed control switch

174. primary, secondary

175. 11

176. N_1 gearbox

177. scavenge

178. airframe

179. reusable

180. accessory gearbox, tank

181. Allison 250

182. C 28, C 30

183. a. compressor
    b. combustor
    c. turbine
    d. accessory gearbox
    e. accessories

184. six stages, centrifugal

185. bleed air, combustor

186. combustor liner, igniter

187. combustor, accessory gearbox

188. two stage, power

189. gas producer turbine, power turbine

190. a. N_1 tachometer .
    b. fuel pump
    c. starter generator
    d. N_1 fuel control

191. a. N_2 tachometer
    b. N_2 governor
    c. torquemeter

192. four

193. oil cooler

194. a. oil pressure regulating valve
    b. filter
    c. differential pressure bypass

195. control valve

196. ground idle

197. Pe

198. diffuser scroll

199. poppet

200. slots, nose

201. a. two spur gear pumps
    b. filter
    c. filter bypass valve
    d. regulator valve
    e. two check valves

202. fuel control

203. twist grip

204. a. cut-off
    b. ground idle
    c. full open

205. discharge pressure

206. starting, ground idle

207. a. regulated air pressure
    b. governor reset pressure
    c. governor servo pressure

208. power turbine

209. droop compensator, beeper button

210. 100%

211. collective

212. gas producer fuel control

213. increased

214. primary

215. a. exciter
    b. spark igniter lead
    c. igniter

216. turbine outlet temperature

217. thermocouples

218. twin pack

219. free power turbines, reduction gearbox

220. three, centrifugal

221. reverse-flow

222. front

223. a. tach generator
    b. fuel control
    c. starter generator

224. accessory gearbox

225. output shaft

226. combining

227. each

228. sprag unit

229. hydropneumatic

230. torque

231. gear

232. power control

233. power

234. torquemeter pressure

235. reset air, equal

236. primary, secondary

237. three

238. output section

239. blowers

240. interstage airbleed

241. #1

242. raised, lowered

243. two output

244. one engine

245. power output

246. rotor

247. airframe

248. a. ground idle
    b. flight idle
    c. full N_1

249. collective

250. airflow

251. engine out

252. cycles

253. modular

254. short shaft

255. shimming

256. flight

257. N_1, N_2

258. twist grip, collective

259. a. shut off valve
    b. idle speed
    c. full automatic power
    d. emergency power control

260. idle stop

261. beep

Answers to Chapter IX

1. anti-torque

2. a. tandem rotors
   b. co-axial rotors
   c. side by side rotors

3. a. pitch change
   b. blade flapping

4. negative, positive

5. foot

6. transmission

7. rotor

8. flexibility

9. hanger bearings

10. vibration

11. gearbox

12. increase

13. increase, decrease

14. faster

15. a. metal
    b. composite

16. hydraulic boost

17. three

18. reduces

19. misalignment

20. greasing

21. universal joint

22. tail rotor gear box, tail boom

23. pitch change

24. acme jack screw

25. bonded metal

26. spherical

27. trunnion, yoke

28. counter weight washers

29. single

30. drive shaft

31. graphite, teflon

32. brass, bonded

33. increaser, decreaser

34. tension torsion strap

35. swashplate

36. honeycomb

37. a. drive fork
    b. teetering bearing
    c. strap pack
    d. flap restrainer

38. tail rotor

39. shims

40. spherical

41. two

42. flexible

43. flexing

44. absorb

45. reduction

46. labyrinth

47. output shaft

48. composites

49. feathering, flapping

50. fiberglass
51. elastomeric
52. tension
53. flex, foam filler
54. 6
55. one
56. curvic
57. static balance
58. 90°
59. front
60. hand packed grease
61. shims
62. lash, pattern
63. reducer
64. shim rings
65. underslung, preconed
66. flex beam
67. uniball, pitch change
68. master blade
69. hydraulic boost
70. temperature
71. high frequency
72. touched
73. stickers

74. rotate
75. pins, rivets
76. disc stacking
77. vibration
78. shims
79. installed
80. shimmed
81. engine lubricant
82. elastomeric
83. finite life
84. high
85. drive system, pitch change
86. statically
87. static, dynamic
88. dangerous
89. tip, blade
90. hub
91. oil
92. collar, disc
93. closed room
94. ball bearing
95. knife edges, roller
96. horizontal
97. dynamic

98. dynamic
99. track
100. normal
101. tip
102. pitch change
103. in, out
104. both
105. tips
106. four
107. superimposed
108. same
109. strobex, vibex
110. vibex
111. target
112. tail rotor
113. clock angle
114. tail rotor
115. calm
116. push pull
117. gradients
118. gradient, magnetic brake
119. extreme
120. pedal
121. too heavy

Answers to Chapter X

1. tubular
2. tolerances
3. monoque, semi monoque
4. tubular, aluminum
5. a. honeycomb
   b. fiberglass
   c. kevlar
6. riveting, welding
7. combination

8. load, stress
9. thrust, lift
10. skid
11. vibration
12. bifilar, nodal beam
13. tail rotor
14. horizontal stabilizer
15. a. skid gear is simple to maintain

b. skid gear is difficult to ground handle
c. wheel gear is more complex
d. wheel gear simplifies ground handling
16. approach
17. main structural
18. lift, thrust, landing loads
19. fuselage

20. X members

21. cabin, body

22. synthetic

23. polycarbonate

24. engine, tail boom

25. frames

26. bolts

27. a. tail rotor gear box
   b. drive shafting
   c. vertical fin
   d. horizontal stabilizer

28. symmetrical, dissymetrical

29. downward

30. ground resonance

31. node, vertical

32. three

33. aluminum

34. a. rigidity
   b. strength
   c. sound proofing

35. tub

36. lift, landing

37. semi-monoque

38. baggage, engine

39. monocoque

40. four bolts

41. unload

42. inverted

43. conventional

44. beam truss

45. center beam

46. a. supports the pilot's floor
   b. supports the pilot's seat
   c. is attached to the forward canted frame
   d. is attached to the rear canted frame

47. mast support

48. box

49. a. seat belts attached to primary structure
   b. a deep fuselage structure
   c. energy absorbing sheet metal seats
   d. truss construction of the cabin section

50. maintenance, structural repair

51. jigs

52. a. rotating components
   b. structure

53. special inspections

54. a. tail boom attach fittings
   b. transmission attachment
   c. engine attachment
   d. gear attachment

55. rotating

56. sudden deceleration of the rotor after contact with an object

57. airframe, rotating

58. a. disassembly and overhaul
   b. rejection of certain parts
   c. rejection of the whole rotor head

59. a. twisting of the tail boom
   b. damage to the hanger bearing mounts
   c. damage to the tail boom mounts

60. tail rotor hub

61. a. fuel systems
   b. electrical systems
   c. heating and air conditioning

62. force feed

63. bladder

64. common

65. electrically

66. two

67. environmental control unit

68. STC's

69. less tail rotor strikes

70. floats

71. external

72. manual, electric

73. exceed

74. be cut

75. not usually